Human Rights

Other titles in the Issues in Focus *series:*

Issues in Focus

Human Rights

Issues for a New Millennium

Linda Jacobs Altman

Enslow Publishers, Inc.

40 Industrial Road   PO Box 38
Box 398   Aldershot
Berkeley Heights, NJ 07922 Hants GU12 6BP
USA   UK

http://www.enslow.com

Library of Congress Cataloging-in-Publication Data

Altman, Linda Jacobs, 1943–
    Human rights : issues for a new millennium / Linda Jacobs
Altman.
        v. cm. — (Issues in focus)
    Summary: Explores the history of concern for human rights around
the world, looking particularly at the internationalism begun in the
last quarter of the twentieth century and its influence on human
rights issues.
    Includes bibliographical references and index.
    Contents: The foundations of human rights— Rights and
revolutions—The struggle against slavery—In time of war—Human
rights and civil disobedience— The activist sixties.
    ISBN 0-7660-1689-7 (hardcover)
    1. Human rights—Juvenile literature. [1. Human rights.] I. Title.
II. Series: Issues in focus (Hillside, N.J.)
JC571 .A384 2002
323—dc21
                                        2002006050

Printed in the United States of America

9 8 7 6 5 4 3 2 1

To Our Readers: We have done our best to make sure all Internet
addresses in this book were active and appropriate when we went to
press. However, the author and the publisher have no control over and
assume no liability for the material available on those Internet sites or
on other Web sites they may link to. Any comments or suggestions can
be sent by e-mail to comments@enslow.com or to the address on the
back cover.

Illustration Credits: Dover Publications, pp. 23, 61; Penelope
D. Klute/VISTA 1968 Chicago, pp. 77, 80; Library of Congress,
pp. 10, 14, 18, 29, 34, 37, 45, 52, 55, 65, 69, 82, 89;
National Archives, pp. 94, 112; Painet Stock Photos, p. 97;
James R. Tourtellotte/U.S. Customs Service, p. 116; UK Ministry
of Defence and Foreign and Commonwealth Office, p. 105.

Cover Illustration: United Nations. Shown is a refugee camp in
Beirut, Lebanon, in 1978.

Contents

1 Human Rights: What They Are and Why They Matter   7

2 The Foundations of Human Rights 12

3 Rights and Revolutions 26

4 The Struggle Against Slavery. . . 36

5 In Time of War 47

6 Human Rights and Civil Disobedience. 60

7 The Activist Sixties 71

8 The New Internationalism 85

9 Unfinished Business 99

Chapter Notes 118

Glossary 123

Further Reading and Internet Addresses 125

Index 126

1

Human Rights: What They Are and Why They Matter

Francis Bok of Sudan was only seven years old when he became a slave. It started in 1986, when Bok's mother sent him to the marketplace to sell eggs and beans. Armed men on horseback attacked the village square, shooting adult men down in the street and grabbing women and children.

Little Francis Bok found himself tied up and slung across the back of a donkey. He was taken north and sold as a slave to an Arab family: "They laughed and called me 'Abeed, abeed'—'black slave,'" Bok remembered. "For ten years, they beat me every morning. They made me sleep with the animals, and they gave me very bad food. They said I was an animal."[1]

After two unsuccessful escape attempts, Bok finally broke free of his master. He made his way to Egypt, where he sought help from the United Nations Refugee Office. In 1999, an American sponsor helped him come to the United States to begin a new life as a free man.

It is hard for many people to believe that slavery still exists in the twenty-first century. But it does. It appears in many parts of the world and in many forms. Wherever it appears, it is an affront to human rights.

Freedom is a core value of human rights—not just freedom from slavery, but from tyranny, oppression, violence, torture, and false imprisonment. Human rights also implies positive freedoms, such as the right to live in dignity, safety, and peace. In short, "human rights" are those rights that all people possess simply because they are human beings.

The term itself is relatively new, having come into general use only after World War II. Americans William Lloyd Garrison and Henry David Thoreau were among the first to use it in anything like its modern sense.

In 1831, antislavery activist Garrison spoke of "defending the great cause of human rights."[2] Thoreau was also speaking of slavery when he called for "the settlement of the question of human rights" in his 1849 essay "Civil Disobedience."[3]

Past generations have more usually talked about

"natural rights," "the rights of man," "God-given rights," or "inalienable rights." By any name, the idea of human rights has been developing over the course of human history and in every culture around the world.

Some eras have produced movements that not only affected the cause of human rights but changed the course of human history. For example, the eighteenth century produced the American and French revolutions, with their passion for liberty and justice. The nineteenth century saw the end of slavery in the United States and many other areas of the world.

The twentieth century was a time of extremes. It saw everything from mass murder and ethnic cleansing to nonviolent social action in the cause of human freedom. It produced brutal dictators like Adolf Hitler and Joseph Stalin and men of peace like Mohandas K. Gandhi and Martin Luther King, Jr. It produced technology that could change the world—or destroy it altogether.

Many issues from the twentieth century and even earlier have continued into the twenty-first. For example, in some parts of the world, widespread slavery still exists. Young children are forced to work long hours for abusive "employers." In some places, women are reduced to the status of nonpersons. The death penalty is becoming increasingly controversial, with opponents claiming that it is legalized murder and should be banned everywhere in the world.

The twenty-first century will also face challenges of its own. For example, rapid growth of communication and computer technology has made privacy an

This drawing from 1942 represents the "four freedoms" that are a part of human rights: freedom of speech, freedom of religion, freedom from want, and freedom from fear.

increasingly important issue. Government or police agencies can monitor every detail of an individual's private life. Criminals can track the movements of potential victims. Even seemingly harmless information gathered from studying patterns of Internet use can be used in ways that violate personal rights.

What may well become the most disturbing issue of the new millennium began on September 11, 2001, when terrorists turned four commercial jetliners into weapons of destruction. After the attack on the World Trade Center in New York City and the Pentagon in Washington, D.C., the United States faced a war against terrorism and the need for heightened security.

This raised profound issues of human rights. How far is too far? Even in countries that harbor terrorists, innocent civilians have the right not to be bombed into oblivion. Even the need for homeland security should not take away individual protections against unreasonable search and seizure.

Nobody knows how these issues will be resolved or what new problems may arise. However, one thing is clear: In this increasingly interconnected world, human rights abuses anywhere will hurt the cause of freedom and personal dignity everywhere.

2

The Foundations of Human Rights

For much of human history, life was short and often brutal. Individual rights were not terribly important in a world where few people lived past the age of thirty. People acquired their rights and responsibilities from membership in families, tribes, social classes, religious organizations, or other groups. The concept of human rights as it is understood today did not exist.

The concept developed slowly, over centuries. Early lawgivers tended to emphasize duties and responsibilities. People owed unquestioning obedience to kings and other leaders. They were supposed to live according to an often elaborate set of rules and regulations. Rights were more likely to be implied than stated. For example, a law against murder implies that human beings have a right to life and personal security. A law against robbery implies property rights.

Dealing with questions of rights and duties was part of the process of building complex civilizations. Small tribal cultures could function without elaborate legal systems. Vast empires could not.

The Code of Hammurabi

The Code of Hammurabi dates from the Babylonian Empire, more than 3,750 years ago. It was long regarded as the first organized statement of law in human history. In the twentieth century, fragments of two earlier codes were found, but Hammurabi's code remains the most useful because it is the most complete.

King Hammurabi ruled the empire of ancient Babylonia from approximately 1792 B.C. to 1750 B.C. In an introduction to the code, Hammurabi explained that he created it "to bring about the rule of righteousness in the land, to destroy the wicked and the evil-doers, so that the strong should not harm the weak."[1]

The code was not a complete legal system. It was basically a list of about three hundred laws, dealing with issues ranging from the penalty for kidnapping or robbery (death) to the fair price for hiring an oxcart and driver (180 *kia* of corn per day).

In criminal matters, Hammurabi's punishments were notably harsh, at least by modern standards. They relied on what is called the *lex talionis*—the famous "eye for an eye" of ancient law. This was not a figurative statement made to illustrate a point. It was an actual law; number 196 in Hammurabi's code: "If a man put out the eye of another man, his eye shall be put out."[2]

In about 1750 B.C., King Hammurabi of the Babylonian Empire established one of the first codes of law.

A son who struck his father would have his hand cut off. Someone who accused another of a capital crime (a crime for which death is the punishment) would himself be put to death if he failed to prove his case.

Hammurabi made few allowances for the offender's motive, intent, or state of mind. There was guilt and there was innocence, with little in between. The idea of degrees of guilt was largely foreign to the legal thinking of the time.

Courts did not consider motive and circumstance. A thief was a thief, whether he stole food for his family or robbed the royal treasury. A killer was a killer, whether he plotted cold-blooded murder or got into a fight and killed someone by accident.

In the history of law, the chief importance of the Code of Hammurabi was in helping to establish rule by law instead of by decree. A decree is a ruling made by someone in authority. It is issued on a case-by-case basis and does not have to conform to any code of law. In government by decree, "law" is whatever the ruling classes decide it should be in any given situation. The Code of Hammurabi was the beginning of an established, consistent approach to justice.

Jewish Law

About four hundred years after Hammurabi, the Hebrew people settled in what is now Israel, bringing with them a law they believed had come directly from God. These "Ten Commandments" were written on stone tablets. They became the foundation for a complete and complex system of laws.

Jewish law was not just a civil code. It was also a religious and moral one. It dealt with government, individual rights and responsibilities, and religious observance. The result was a way of life that has endured in some ways to the present day.

One reason Judaism has survived for so long is its ability to change with the times. In 1300 B.C., Jewish civil law had much in common with the Code of Hammurabi. Both condoned slavery. Both based punishments on the *lex talionis*.

As Jewish law developed, it did away with slavery and replaced the "eye for an eye" doctrine with the concept of money damages. A person who injured another in some way would pay that person an amount of money to compensate for the damage. Jewish law also created safeguards to protect the rights of the accused. The principle underlying these changes was the belief that every life was precious in the sight of God.

The Talmud, Jewish religious writings, says that "whosoever saves one life, it is as if he had saved the whole human race."[3] Preserving life was more important than keeping religious law. For example, a doctor could break the prohibition about working on the Sabbath in order to treat a seriously ill patient. This reverence for life was perhaps ancient Judaism's greatest legacy to what would later be called "human rights."

Greek Law and the Birth of Democracy

The civilization of ancient Greece was secular rather than religious. The Greeks had many gods, but they honored reason and the quest for knowledge above any of them. They produced more statesmen and philosophers than prophets and priests.

Instead of vast empires, they produced the small and self-contained *polis*, or city-state. Instead of monarchy, rule by kings, they developed a revolutionary new political system: democracy. The word comes from the Greek *demos*, "people," and *krateein*, "to rule."

Greek democracy was different from the modern form found in countries such as the United States. The American system is based on free elections of representatives. These representatives do the actual work of making law and public policy. In the Greek polis, citizens participated directly in the decision-making process.

This sort of hands-on government would have been impossible in an empire like Babylonia or Egypt. It was perfectly suited to the polis. The largest of these city-states, Athens, was about the size of Rhode Island. Its population numbered in the thousands, not the millions. Athenian democracy survived for almost two hundred years. Its influence lasted even longer. The philosophy and law of Athens and the other Greek city-states was spread throughout the Western world by the Roman Empire.

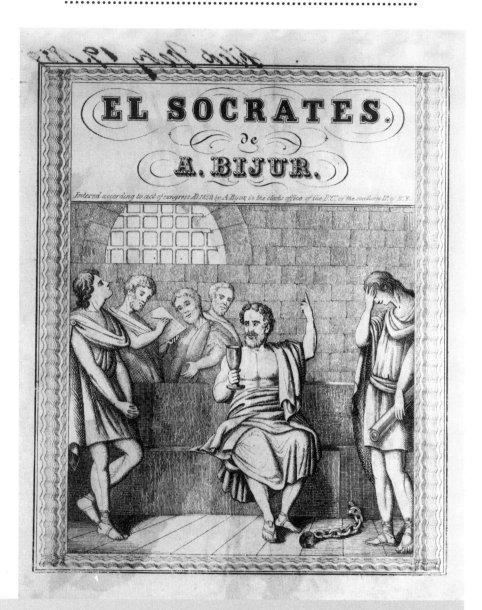

Socrates (470–399 B.C.) was the most influential of the ancient Greek philosophers. He urged people to think about how best to live a moral life.

The Roman Empire

At the height of its power, the Roman Empire stretched from Britain to the Black Sea. Its territory included most of continental Europe, the Mediterranean, the Middle East, and parts of western Asia and north Africa. For sheer size and power, human history had never seen its like.

Rome began as a small city-state populated by wealthy landholders, or *patricians*, free peasants known as *plebeians*, and a large number of slaves. On the road to empire it first became a republic.

The "Law of the Twelve Tables" was the legal foundation of the republic. This code, written around 450 B.C., established rules of evidence and courtroom procedure that have endured to the present day in the court system of the United States and many other countries. It laid the foundation for the right to due process of law (trial according to rules that protect legal rights) with one sentence: "Putting to death . . . of any man who has not been convicted [found guilty], whosoever he might be, is forbidden."[4]

Many of the laws of the republic carried over into the period of empire, which began in 27 B.C. The Romans built their empire as warriors and conquerors. They ruled it as skilled administrators rather than brutal overlords.

Their liberal policy in occupied lands was well known throughout the ancient world. They extended Roman citizenship to conquered peoples. Instead of imposing their own laws, they developed the principle of *jus gentium*, or "law of the peoples."

According to *jus gentium*, certain laws were fundamental to the human condition. They applied equally to all people in every place and time. So long as these universal laws were obeyed, the provinces could govern themselves as they saw fit. According to *The Catholic Encyclopedia*, the basic principles of the *jus gentium* were "to live honestly, not to injure another, to give unto each one his due."[5]

These policies did not solve all problems or stop all conflicts. There was still an emperor in Rome, whose power was above both law and government policy. If he was cruel and tyrannical, the people suffered. There was a bureaucracy, or system of administration, that entangled government in an ever-growing web of rules and procedures.

The Christian Way

While Rome still ruled most of the known world, a new tradition was born in what is now considered the Middle East. A humble teacher dared to confront both Roman and Jewish authorities with a message of love and peace. The teachings of Jesus focused on how human beings should relate to one another and to God. He talked about forgiveness and answering hatred with love. He told his followers to be peacemakers.

Jesus was a spiritual teacher rather than a human rights activist. Still, his teachings helped to shape Christian ideas of human rights. For example, the Sermon on the Mount teaches qualities such as righteousness, meekness, purity of heart, and mercy.

Underlying these virtues is respect for life and for the humanity of every individual.

Human Rights in Medieval Europe

The fall of the Roman Empire is usually dated from 476 A.D., when a warlike people called the Huns deposed, or ousted, the emperor from his throne in Rome. After that time, the Roman Catholic Church and the feudal state began to become the most powerful institutions in Europe.

In feudalism, wealthy aristocrats controlled vast lands. These estates were like miniature kingdoms, with the lord of the manor holding absolute power over the land and everyone on it.

Medieval aristocrats did not work for a living. They fought the wars and administered justice on their lands. Having a job would be beneath their station.

The aristocrats' lands supported them. They collected rent and taxes from craftsmen and free peasants who lived as tenants on their property. They used serfs to cultivate crops and raise livestock for the needs of the manor itself.

Serfs were little better off than slaves. They were not owned by the lord of the manor, but they were tied for life to the land. They were no more free to leave than the livestock, nor could they have any property of their own. Serfs had no rights, only such privileges as the lord of the manor decided to give them. He could take away those privileges at any time and for any reason.

The aristocracy in turn owed unquestioning

obedience to the king: an absolute monarch whose word was law. In theory, the king himself was answerable only to God. In practice, this meant that even kings had to respect the authority of the Church.

As God's representative on earth, the Church held absolute authority in spiritual matters—great authority indeed in medieval Europe. The hope of Heaven and the threat of Hell were very real to people of all social classes, from the lowliest serf to the mightiest king.

In a culture dominated by the monarchy and the Church, obedience was a great virtue. People were expected to obey the king in worldly matters and the Church in spiritual ones. Society as a whole was not much concerned with issues such as personal freedom and individual rights.

That began to change in 1215. A group of English nobles rebelled against the policies of King John. Among other things, he had launched disastrous territorial wars and burdened the nobility with taxes to pay for them. Many of the nobles felt that stopping the king was the only way to save England.

The result of their rebellion was the Magna Carta, one of the founding documents of human rights in the West. The English nobles forced King John to sign it in June 1215. It curbed the power of the king and established the principle of rule by law rather than royal decree.

The Magna Carta limited the king's right to impose taxes, levy fees, or take property. It gave legal protection to people accused of crimes by banning

Servant   Pope of Rome   King

During the Middle Ages, even kings were supposed to be obedient to the Church. Shown are a servant, pope, and king of the twelfth century, before the signing of the Magna Carta.

arrest without evidence and imprisonment without trial. In conclusion, the king agreed "that all these above mentioned provisions shall be observed with good faith and without evil intent."[6]

The Magna Carta did not create an entirely new form of government, nor did it deal with the rights of the masses. However, the principles behind it had far-reaching effects throughout English and European society.

Human Rights in Non-Western Cultures

Eastern cultures also produced religious, philosophical, and legal systems that served as later foundations for human rights. Some of these traditions did not emphasize the individual to the degree found in the West. However, they shared one important characteristic: respect for life, especially human life.

The Chinese philosopher Confucius (551–479 B.C.) based an entire moral system on the idea that humankind is basically good. He emphasized duty to family and, by extension, to the entire human family.

In India, Gautama Buddha (563–483 B.C.) valued the ways of peace. He taught the equality of all people and was opposed to slavery in any form. Buddhism's respect for life extended beyond human beings to include all creatures.

The prophet Muhammad (A.D. 570–632) founded Islam in the Middle East; his followers are called Muslims. Islam soon spread to parts of Asia and Africa as well. Islamic culture became well-known for its tolerance of other beliefs. Christians, Jews, and others could worship in their own way and direct their own affairs. Many non-Muslims served in high positions at the court of the sultan, or ruler.

Tribal cultures in Africa, the Americas, and other places tend to be overlooked in discussions about human rights. Yet many of them developed traditions that were the equal of anything in Europe or Asia. For example, the Iroquois League of North America was a confederation of five large tribes. Long before European settlers arrived, the League created a democratic constitution that became one of the models for the U.S. Constitution.

East or West, ideas of human rights were rooted in principles of law, justice, and respect for life. These concepts developed slowly in the ancient world. In time, respect for life was broadened to include personal freedom and individual rights. These ideas would in turn inspire revolutions that would one day make even more profound changes.

3

Rights and Revolutions

On a cold December night in 1773, a group of American colonists dressed as Mohawk Indians and blackened their faces with coal dust. Armed with hatchets and clubs, they made their way to Boston Harbor. There, they boarded three British cargo ships.

Their mission was to destroy a large shipment of tea to protest the import tax imposed by Britain. One of the participants, George Hewes, later wrote about his experiences:

> When we arrived at the wharf, there were three of our number who assumed an authority to

direct our operations. . . . They divided us into three parties, for the purpose of boarding the three ships which contained the tea at the same time. . . . We were then ordered by our commander to open the hatches and take out all the chests of tea and throw them overboard . . . first cutting and splitting the chests with our [hatchets], so as thoroughly to expose them to the effects of the water.[1]

Sixteen months later, on April 19, 1775, the American Revolution began.

Some of the most stirring human rights declarations in history have come out of revolutions. For example, the English Revolution of 1689, the American Revolution of 1776, and the French Revolution of 1789 each produced a bill of rights. These codes of law protected individual freedom within the society.

The English Bill of Rights

The English Bill of Rights grew out of what came to be known as the Glorious Revolution. This 1688–1689 revolt brought down a king and transformed the British government into a democracy. It also did away with a peculiar doctrine known as "the divine right of kings."

Divine right held that kings received their authority directly from God. Therefore, they could not be held accountable to any human agency. To oppose a king—even a bad one—was to sin against God himself.

James II treated divine right as a license. He

dismissed judges of the High Court, dissolved Parliament, and appointed unqualified and dishonest men to high posts in the government. When bishops of the Anglican Church tried to present a petition of grievances and concerns, James had them arrested and imprisoned.

By 1689, even believers in divine right had decided they would rather sin than continue to endure James's rule. The philosopher John Locke added fuel to the fires of rebellion, arguing that human beings have a right to revolt against oppression.

In Locke's view, government was a contract between the ruler and the ruled. A ruler who failed to keep his part of the bargain had broken the contract. Therefore, he could—and should—be deposed.

After the Glorious Revolution forced James from the throne, Locke's ideas helped to lay the groundwork for the English Bill of Rights. Its provisions included freedom of speech, the right to vote in parliamentary elections, and protection against cruel and unusual punishment. Nearly a hundred years later, those principles would reappear in the founding documents of the United States and the French Republic.

The American Experiment in Democracy

The watchword of the American Revolutionary War was "liberty," or "freedom." Freedom was considered a natural right of humankind, as Thomas Jefferson so eloquently stated in the famous lines of the

Declaration of Independence: "We hold these truths to be self-evident, that all men are created equal, that they are endowed by their Creator with certain unalienable Rights, that among these are Life, Liberty and the pursuit of Happiness."

In these few words, the Declaration set the tone for the American definition of freedom. It differed from older definitions in one all-important way: The right to freedom was based upon the foundation of human equality. Historian Eric Foner called that "a truly radical principle, whose full implications no one could anticipate."[2]

More than one hundred years after the Revolutionary War, an artist drew this cartoon depicting the Battle of Bunker Hill, showing the American colonists, armed with farm tools, defeating the British.

The Declaration of Independence did not give hard-and-fast definitions of liberty, equality, and the pursuit of happiness. It described an ideal rather than a finished system. The democracy of the Declaration was a work in progress, to be shaped and defined by the American people.

The work began at the Constitutional Convention of 1787. The delegates arrived in Philadelphia knowing they faced a long and difficult process.

Slavery was the most controversial issue. The South wanted it, but the North did not. To create a constitution that everyone could support, the delegates had to compromise.

The North agreed not to ban the Atlantic slave trade for twenty years. A fugitive slave law provided for escaped slaves to be returned to their "rightful owners."

James Madison of Virginia argued for the compromise by assuring his fellow Southerners that the institution of slavery was well protected. He was right. It would be seventy-eight years before the United States finally abolished slavery.

The Bill of Rights

Today, the Bill of Rights is so important to American freedom that it is difficult to imagine a time without it. Yet in 1787, many people thought a formal statement of rights was unnecessary or perhaps even harmful.

Most of the framers accepted the doctrine of natural rights. By definition, these rights were part of the human condition. Government had no right to grant them or take them away. Therefore, creating a bill of rights would overstep governmental authority. In addition, a list that reserved specific rights to the people might imply that unnamed rights belonged to the government.

Problems such as these were the chief reason that no statement of rights appeared in the body of the Constitution. The ten amendments that became known as the Bill of Rights were hotly debated for two years before they were finally ratified into law on December 15, 1791. In its final form, the Bill of Rights recognized rights that were not natural in themselves, but that served to protect natural rights. For example, freedom of the press did not exist in nature, but it was a necessary extension of the right to free speech. Trial by jury was not a natural right, but it protected the life, liberty, and property of those accused of crimes.

James Madison, the Virginian who had engineered the compromise over slavery, also shepherded the Bill of Rights through Congress. Madison was personally torn over the question of slavery. Though he believed it was immoral to treat any human being as property, he owned many slaves.

Perhaps because of his own conflicts, Madison realized that any statement of rights needed room to evolve. He was largely responsible for the Ninth and Tenth amendments that together provided a "safety valve" for unnamed rights.

The Ninth Amendment states: "The enumeration [listing] in the Constitution of certain rights shall not be construed to deny or disparage [discredit] others retained by the people." The Tenth Amendment directly limits the federal government to named rights: "The powers not delegated to the United States by the Constitution, nor prohibited by it to the states, are reserved to the states respectively, or to the people."

"Liberty, Equality, Fraternity"— The French Revolution

The French Revolution of 1789 brought the battle for democracy to continental Europe. At the time, France had the largest population in Europe but was unable to produce enough food for everyone. In the cities and in the countryside, poor people starved to death, while feudal lords enjoyed their vast estates. A rising middle class was denied the right to participate in government.

The mood of the country grew increasingly restless as the lower and middle classes pressed for change. While the rulers hesitated, the people starved. This led to the Great Fear of July 1789 as peasants panicked and troops surrounded Paris.

On July 14, 1789, a mob stormed the Bastille, a fortress-prison in Paris. In the countryside, peasants rose up against their lords. What began as a disorganized revolt by starving masses was turning into a full-scale revolution.

A National Assembly formed by revolutionaries met to create a new constitution. On August 27, 1789, the assembly adopted the Declaration of the

Rights of Man and of the Citizen. This document was a ringing affirmation of freedom. Its definition of political liberty was firmly based in the doctrine of natural rights, saying, "Political liberty consists in the power of doing whatever does not injure another." The only limits on the "natural rights" of any person were those that were necessary to allow every other person "the free exercise of the same rights."[3]

This was more democracy than King Louis XVI could take. He refused to sanction, or approve, the new laws. This set into motion a series of events that would tear France apart.

On January 21, 1793, Louis XVI was beheaded before a cheering crowd of revolutionaries. A year and a half later, France entered the period that came to be known as the Reign of Terror.

The high ideals of the Declaration of the Rights of Man and the Citizen went by the wayside. The revolutionary government rounded up about three hundred thousand people suspected of royalist sympathies. Seventeen thousand were guillotined after unfair "show" trials. Thousands more died in prison or were simply killed without even the pretense of a trial.

The royalists fought back. In October 1795, they tried to retake Paris. The effort was quashed by an ambitious young general named Napoleon Bonaparte.

The Napoleonic Code

Napoleon Bonaparte was part military adventurer, part lawgiver, and part ruthless conqueror. In his

Because King Louis XVI of France refused to grant the revolutionaries' demands for liberty and democracy, he was beheaded. This was followed by the Reign of Terror, in which thousands of aristocrats and others loyal to the monarchy were sent to the guillotine.

boundless ambition, he aimed to conquer the world. This he did not do, but in the process of trying, he spread the principles of the revolution throughout Europe. In every conquered nation, he established the legal system that came to be known as the Napoleonic Code.

Before the revolution, French law had been a hodgepodge of royal decrees, local regulations, and laws left over from Roman times. Feudal lords owed allegiance to the king but otherwise regulated their estates as they saw fit. On his own lands, a lord's word was quite literally the law.

In 1804, the Napoleonic Code established one

legal system that was the same for all people in all places. Thus, it opened the way for greater social, economic, and religious freedom for all citizens.

The legal codes that grew out of revolutions in England, the United States, and France were united by a common bond: freedom. To build a free society it is necessary to safeguard individual rights. The seventeenth and eighteenth centuries saw the end of feudalism and serfdom in Western Europe, the rise of democracy, and a new emphasis on the dignity and worth of every individual. The nineteenth century would face one of the most difficult human rights issues of all: the institution of human slavery.

4

The Struggle Against Slavery

Being a slave meant being property, like a farm tool or an animal. Slaves had no rights, no possessions, no freedom of choice. They could not choose what sort of work to do, where to live, whom to marry. In many places and times, they could be starved, beaten, even killed, and their masters would not be held responsible.

The institution of slavery has existed since the beginning of recorded history, and probably before. When nations made war on one another, the victors looted the resources of their conquered enemies.

They took gold, jewels, and anything else of value—including captives. These captives became slaves.

The Business of Slavery

In the ancient world, slavery was usually a by-product of war and conquest. In the mid-fifteenth century, it became a business. The Atlantic slave trade, as it came to be called, began with Portuguese seamen who sailed to Africa in search of gold and returned with slaves instead.

On August 8, 1444, about six ships made landfall on the Portuguese coast. The sailors began offloading their cargo: 235 slaves. The captives were

For nearly four hundred years, slaves were transported to the Americas from Africa. Chained up in the dark, with inadequate food, water, or fresh air, thousands of the captives died.

stunned and terrified. Portuguese nobleman Gomes Eannes de Zurata wrote:

> What heart could be so hard as not to be pierced with . . . feeling to see that company? For some kept their heads low, and their faces bathed in tears, looking one upon another. Others stood groaning . . . [or] struck their faces with the palms of their hands . . . while others made lamentations in the manner of a dirge [a funeral chant].[1]

From that sad but small beginning, the Atlantic slave trade grew to become one of the biggest business enterprises in human history. The opening of the Americas to exploration and settlement provided a ready market for black slaves from Africa. Between 1492 and 1870, about 11 million people were snatched from their homes and shipped to the Americas. The trade reached its height in the 1780s— the same decade that gave birth to the American Bill of Rights and the French Declaration of the Rights of Man and the Citizen.

Slavery and Racism

In America, many of the patriots who fought for their own rights continued to own slaves. To quiet moral qualms over this uncomfortable fact, they resorted to racism. They convinced themselves that blacks were naturally inferior to whites.

This belief allowed slave traders to do their jobs without guilt or pity. It allowed masters to treat their slaves more like livestock than human beings and whites in general to set themselves apart from blacks.

It also allowed the Founding Fathers of American democracy to exclude African slaves from the protections of the Constitution. In a 1973 speech to the House Judiciary Committee, Barbara Jordan, the first African-American woman from a Southern state to serve in Congress, reflected on the meaning of this:

> Earlier today we heard the beginning of the Preamble to the Constitution of the United States, *We, the people*. It is a very eloquent beginning. But when that document was completed, on the seventeenth of September in 1787, I was not included in that *We, the people*. I felt somehow for many years that George Washington and Alexander Hamilton just left me out by mistake. But through the process of amendment, interpretation, and court decision I have finally been included in *We, the people*.[2]

The struggle to include African Americans in the rights of citizenship lasted more than ninety years and ended in a bloody civil war. Along the way, many brave people, African-American and white, worked for the cause of human rights and human freedom.

The End of the Slaving Ships

The first step toward ending slavery was ending the Atlantic slave trade. This was not an easy task. The buying and selling of Africans was an immensely profitable business in the United States, Great Britain, and several other nations.

Despite this profitability, active abolition societies on both sides of the Atlantic sought to end the trafficking in human lives. They began by mobilizing public opinion against the brutal conditions on slaving ships. They lobbied government officials and held protests and rallies. They made speeches and wrote books and articles. These methods would later become some of the strongest weapons of the entire human rights movement.

The captain and crew of the British ship *Zong* unwittingly helped the abolitionists prove their point. In September 1781, the *Zong* became lost at sea with 442 slaves aboard. As supplies of drinking water ran low, the captives began to sicken and die.

Captain Luke Collingswood was determined to save the situation for the wealthy owners of his ship. He knew that insurance would not pay for people who died naturally during the voyage. However, it would pay for cargo that had to be scuttled for the safety of the ship. He therefore ordered that more than a hundred sick or dying people be thrown alive into the sea.

Back in England, the insurance company refused to pay for the loss. Its representatives did not question the captain's right to kill so many people. They only questioned his motive. The water situation was not critical, they said; Collingswood was simply trying to cut his employer's losses by shifting financial responsibility to the insurance company.

Abolitionist attorney Granville Sharp tried to have Collingswood charged with murder. The British Admiralty Court would not allow it. Solicitor General John Lee scolded Sharp for his "pretended appeal to humanity," and declared that a master could drown slaves without "[any] impropriety."[3]

The public was shocked by this judgment. Even many slave owners believed that their human property had at least a right to life. Executing a slave for some crime was one thing; killing the innocent was quite another.

The *Zong* tragedy helped rally public opinion against the slave trade. In 1807, both the United States and Great Britain outlawed the Atlantic trade. Neither of these laws banned slavery as an institution. Within each country buying, selling, and owning slaves was still entirely legal. Importing new slaves from Africa was not, though illegal trafficking continued for many years.

In the Cause of Freedom

Outlawing the international trade was only the beginning of what would become a long and bloody struggle. In 1833, Great Britain passed a law to abolish slavery in its Caribbean colonies. This law freed about eight hundred thousand enslaved Africans who worked on the vast sugar plantations of the islands.

In the United States, 1833 saw the founding of a new group: the American Anti-Slavery Society. It was led by William Lloyd Garrison, a white newspaper editor with a passion for social reform. Garrison believed that slavery was a moral issue rather than an economic or political one. It grew out of white racism and bigotry. He called upon whites to go beyond their prejudices and recognize the common humanity that links all people together.

This belief in African-American equality did not sit well with many people. Even within the ranks of the abolitionist movement, there were whites who were as racially bigoted as any Southern slave owner. They opposed slavery, but considered blacks a "lower order" of humanity. The idea of equal rights for former slaves was unthinkable to them.

William Lloyd Garrison was aware of this attitude. He simply refused to yield to it. Equality to him was an absolute value. He welcomed both blacks and women into full voting membership in the Anti-Slavery Society. This policy eventually split the organization.

In spite of infighting, the abolitionists raised public consciousness about slavery. Towering figures such as former slave Frederick Douglass and the fiery "Quaker maid" Abby Kelley gave voice to the issues. They won hearts and minds in the North and in the new Western territories. The South did not budge.

War and Emancipation

When Abraham Lincoln was elected president in 1860, the fragile peace that held the nation together was shattered. The people of the South regarded Lincoln as an antislavery candidate. Therefore, his election served notice that the Southern way of life was in jeopardy.

On December 20, 1860, South Carolina became the first state to secede (withdraw) from the Union.

Others soon followed. Even before Lincoln's inauguration on March 4, 1861, the breakaway states formed their own government, called the Confederate States of America. After that, war was not long in coming. The first battle began on April 12, 1861, at Fort Sumter, South Carolina.

Both sides believed they were fighting for freedom. The North fought to preserve the Union as "the beacon light of liberty and freedom to the human race," in the words of one young soldier.[4] The South fought for local self-government and property rights—with "property" including both land and slaves.

The war lasted for four long and bloody years. When it ended, the South was shattered, the slaves were free, and the American nation faced a long period of healing.

Reconstruction and African-American Rights

After the war and continuing until 1877, Union troops occupied the South. This period of Reconstruction was supposed to accomplish two things: rebuild the Southern economy, which had been devastated by the war, and help liberated slaves adjust to their new freedom.

The foundation of that freedom was built into the U.S. Constitution. Congress passed three amendments to ensure the rights of former slaves. The Thirteenth Amendment abolished the institution of slavery from American life. The Fourteenth

Amendment guaranteed American citizenship and "equal protection of the law" to all people born in the United States, regardless of race. The Fifteenth Amendment prohibited the states from making race a qualification for voting.

Backed by the grandeur of the U.S. Constitution, the early days of Reconstruction seemed full of promise. As historian Leon F. Litwack noted, "It was a time of unparalleled hope, laden with possibility, when black men and women acted to shape their own destiny."[5]

Unfortunately, equality under the law did not mean equality in everyday life. Grinding poverty became its own form of slavery. The freedmen, as they were called, had to work long and hard simply to stay alive. Many became field hands or sharecroppers on the same plantations where they had been slaves. They had neither the time nor the resources to enjoy their freedom.

African Americans were victimized by employment practices that kept them as near to slavery as possible. For example, they had to agree to year-long employment contracts at wages barely high enough to live on. There were severe penalties for failure to fulfill those contracts. Under this system, the employer no longer owned his workers, but he did own their time.

Reconstruction ended after a disputed presidential election in 1876. In order to get enough electoral votes to become president, Rutherford B. Hayes had to agree to remove all Union troops from the South. When they had gone, Reconstruction came to an abrupt end.

During the period of Reconstruction after the Civil War, efforts were made to help freed slaves adjust to their new lives. Shown is a member of the Freedman's Bureau trying to separate groups of angry whites and African Americans.

The Rise of Jim Crow

"Jim Crow" was the name of a popular minstrel-show character. He was a stumbling, bumbling African-American man, played by a white performer in "blackface" makeup. Nobody seems to know exactly how this character became the symbol of racial segregation in the South.

Jim Crow stood for public facilities such as lunch counters, water fountains, and restrooms marked "colored" and "white." It stood for segregated schools and churches, for theaters with a "colored section" in the topmost balcony, and for buses where African-American people had to sit in the back.

African Americans in a Jim Crow world had no rights that could not be taken away. They were terrorized by the "night riders" of the Ku Klux Klan: men with white robes and hoods who beat, burned, flogged, and lynched—illegally executed—African American people who "got out of line."

In the 1890s, 1,217 African Americans were lynched for "crimes" ranging from trying to vote to arguing with a white man about the price of blackberries. By the turn of the twentieth century, it was clear that the promise of Reconstruction had failed. In its place was Jim Crow segregation and the knowledge that the African-American struggle for human rights had just begun.

5

In Time of War

The first half of the twentieth century saw two world wars and a revolution that established a Communist dictatorship in Russia. These conflicts not only involved the merciless repression of human rights, but the attempted extermination of whole peoples.

From the Armenian death marches in Turkey during World War I to the extermination camps of Nazi Germany in World War II, millions of innocent civilians lost their lives. Millions more were persecuted, imprisoned, or tortured for real or imagined offenses against the state.

47

War and Human Rights

It is no accident that some of the worst human rights violations in history have occurred in time of war. War tends to make hatred of that nameless, faceless horror called "the enemy" seem like a patriotic duty. On the battlefield, that hatred makes the killing easier.

Off the battlefield, it can lead to brutality and violence against prisoners of war, enemy civilians in occupied territories, and minority groups at home.

Minorities have often fared badly in wartime. This is especially true of those who bear—or are thought to bear—some connection to the enemy. For example, when the United States was at war with Japan in World War II, the loyalties of Japanese Americans became suspect. Thousands of people of Japanese descent were put into detention camps to wait out the war. Many Chinese Americans and others of Asian descent faced harassment because of their Asian features.

After the September 11, 2001, terrorist attacks on the United States, many Arab Americans faced discrimination and harassment in various forms. On October 1, the *Detroit Free Press* reported:

> More than 40 percent of local Arab Americans said they know personally of someone who has experienced an act of bias recently because of their Middle Eastern ancestry. Those acts ranged from strange looks and nasty comments to threats and the vandalizing of cars by scratching them with keys.[1]

The Armenian Genocide

During World War I, the government of the Ottoman, or Turkish, Empire was at war with neighboring Russia. The Turkish government became suspicious about the loyalties of its Armenian minority because many of them had connections to the Armenian community in Russia. The result was the first genocide of the twentieth century.

The word *genocide* did not yet exist. It would be coined after World War II, to describe the systematic slaughter of whole peoples. In genocide, people are massacred simply because of their membership in a particular racial, religious, ethnic, or national group. The term was first used to describe Nazi Germany's attempt to exterminate, or completely destroy, the Jews of Europe.

Though the word did not appear until after World War II, the idea behind it certainly existed. According to the Armenian National Institute in Washington, D.C., the Turks killed about a million and a half Armenians between 1915 and 1923.[2]

Armenians all over the world mark April 24, 1915, as the day the terror began. On that day, the government arrested hundreds of Armenian intellectuals and community leaders in Constantinople (present-day Istanbul). These people were later killed, along with five thousand ordinary Armenians who were snatched off the streets or taken from their homes.

Weeks before the Constantinople massacre, the Turks had quietly disarmed all Armenian soldiers in their army. Some of the Armenians were put to work on road gangs. Others were used almost as pack animals, to carry supplies.

As educators Donald E. Miller and Lorna Touryan Miller explained, the Armenians

> were poorly fed and clothed, and the goal of working them until they dropped from hunger and exhaustion soon became evident. With few exceptions, those who did not die in this manner were taken in groups of fifty or one hundred and shot, often after having been forced to dig their own graves.[3]

When the community leaders were dead and the soldiers disarmed, the death marches began. Armenians were taken from their homes and force marched toward prison camps deep in the desert. Thousands died before reaching their destination.

The Turks took violent criminals from the prisons to act as guards. These men drove the marchers relentlessly, killing those who fell by the wayside. They looked the other way when thieves on horseback attacked and robbed helpless marchers.

Every day, people died. Those who survived the marches were put into camps where many more died of hunger, thirst, or exposure to the burning desert sun. By the end of the war in 1918, there was scarcely an Armenian survivor who had not lost someone near and dear.

In spite of this, the Turkish government denied that the genocide ever happened. They claimed they were simply removing the Armenians from the war zone.

The world largely ignored the fate of Turkey's Armenian minority. A few religious and charitable organizations helped refugees, especially the thousands of children orphaned by the war. These groups could shelter, feed, and clothe the survivors. They did not have the power to bring the perpetrators to justice. Neither did the League of Nations, forerunner of the United Nations.

The Communist Takeover in Russia

Just two years after the Armenian genocide began, Russia was caught up in a bloody revolutionary war. The October Revolution of 1917 deposed the czar, or emperor, and put the Communist Party in power. Russia became the core nation of the Union of Soviet Socialist Republics, or the Soviet Union.

In theory, the Soviet Union was a "classless" society in which all people would be equal and private property would be abolished. Everything would be owned in common by the people (the citizens of the Soviet Union). Farms and factories would be "collectivized," with large numbers of people living and working together in government-owned facilities.

In practice, this meant that the Soviet government controlled the whole economy. All able-bodied citizens were expected to work. In return, they received necessities such as housing, food, medical care, and clothing.

The system produced equality at the cost of variety and individual choice. The result was a dreary regimentation. Individuals became little more

Following the Russian Revolution of 1917, the Soviet economy was controlled by the state at the expense of individual rights. Shown are men and women working on the railroad tracks near Petrograd in 1922.

than cogs in the great Soviet machine. To keep them in line, the government trampled on human rights.

The Bolsheviks, as the revolutionaries were called, killed the royal family and every member of the nobility they could find. Then they started on wealthy property owners. Anyone who owned a factory, for example, was automatically an exploiter of the proletariat, or working class. The government stripped these people of their property and either killed them on the spot or sent them to labor camps, where many died of starvation and overwork.

The process of collectivization went on for a number of years. By the summer of 1932, Soviet dictator Joseph Stalin was ready to concentrate on the *kulaks*. These were land-owning Ukrainian peasants who had not taken kindly to the idea of collectivization. For the "crime" of preferring their own land to a collective farm, Stalin decided to starve them to death.

In the summer of 1932, Stalin ordered Ukrainian farmers to deliver 6.6 million tons of grain from the next harvest. This was an impossible demand. Stalin knew full well that the farmers could never meet it. He did not care. It was not grain he wanted, but an excuse to punish farmers who failed to meet their quota. A second order declared every crop in Ukraine to be government property.

These two orders were nothing less than a death sentence for millions of people. According to historian James Mace, "Anyone who so much as gleaned an ear of grain or bit the root off a sugar beet was to be considered an enemy of the people subject to execution."[4]

When the expected quota failure occurred, the government moved swiftly to seize the entire harvest. Communist officials in Ukraine dispatched special troops to make sure the peasants were not hoarding food. These brigades searched houses and barns, root cellars, storerooms, and anywhere else food might be hidden.

By the winter of 1932–1933, people were dying. They died by the hundreds of thousands; so many that survivors could not bury all the bodies. As many as 10 million starved to death during that terrible winter. Nearly 10 million more were deported to labor camps in Siberia.

Ukraine was collectivized as Stalin had wanted. In little more than a year, the dictator had stripped the Ukrainian people of their land, their livelihood, and even their right to life itself. The Soviet people saw the horror and looked the other way.

Many acted out of fear. Others needed to believe that communism would indeed produce a society without class distinctions. It would be a "workers' paradise" in which all people were comrades and no one lacked for the necessities of life. As former general Petro Grigorenko explained, "We believed so strongly in communism that we [would] accept any crime if it was glossed over with the least little bit of Communist phraseology."[5]

The Nazi "Racial State"

While Stalin was starving the Ukrainians into submission, another dictator was on the rise. On January 30, 1933, Adolf Hitler was appointed chancellor of Germany. His National Socialist, or Nazi, party promoted an openly racist brand of ultranationalism. It would lead to war and genocide.

Hitler envisioned a racial state ruled by a "master race" of tall, blond, blue-eyed Northern Europeans, or Aryans, as he called them. They would be a warrior people, proving themselves through struggle and conflict.

The best of them would fight their way to

positions of leadership. Even the humblest would be entitled by birth to dominate "inferior races" such as Jews, Poles, Russians, and all people of color. These "subhumans" would have no future in the world the Nazis planned. Millions would be exterminated. Those left alive would have no rights at all. They would exist only to serve their Nazi masters.

Not even "Aryans" would be free in Hitler's Germany. Hitler planned for them to march through life in lockstep, their every thought and action

Adolf Hitler (at left), shown here with his aides, promoted a brand of racist ultranationalism in Germany that led to war and genocide—the attempt to eradicate an entire people.

controlled by an all-powerful state. There would be Nazi-sponsored social and professional clubs to keep them busy and pomp and pageantry to fire their patriotism. There would be a large and powerful network of state police to keep the people obedient.

Less than a month after becoming chancellor, Hitler used an arson, or deliberately set fire, at a government building to whip the nation into an anti-Communist frenzy. When a known Communist sympathizer was arrested for the crime, Hitler claimed it was the beginning of a Communist plot to take over the country. He needed power to act before it was too late.

He convinced the elderly and ailing German president, Paul von Hindenburg, to grant him that power. On February 28, 1933, von Hindenburg issued a decree that "suspended freedom of assembly and expression, authorised wiretaps and opening of mail, and sanctioned search and indefinite detention without warrants," as British historian Michael Burleigh explained. "This formed the basis of police power, until the police became so powerful that they eventually required no written authorisation at all."[6]

After von Hindenburg died, Hitler proclaimed himself führer, or absolute leader, of the German nation. From there, he went on to create the most murderous empire of the twentieth century. The Nazi Reich, or empire, was supposed to last for a thousand years. It lasted twelve.

In that short time, the Nazis produced another world war and built a German society based on terror and killing. They arrested people who opposed them and put them into concentration camps. There, these prisoners were starved and mistreated and forced to work long hours for the Nazis.

To build their German "master race," the Nazis claimed the right of life and death over millions. They sterilized people with inherited defects to prevent them from having children. They killed newborn babies with handicaps and older people with mental retardation or mental illness. They killed 6 million European Jews and at least 5 million others who belonged to groups they considered "subhuman."

When the Second World War ended in 1945, even battle-hardened soldiers were shocked by the carnage they saw. Nazis who participated in the killing were put on trial for crimes against humanity. Many were sentenced to death for their part in the genocide.

International Solutions

The Nuremberg Trials, named after the German city in which they were held, became a landmark in international law. Never before had different countries come together to form a court of justice. Never before had the leaders of a nation been held accountable for "crimes against humanity"—acts of brutality and murder that went beyond the scope of warfare.

For such terrible crimes, punishing the guilty did not seem to be enough. The Holocaust, as it came to be called, did not only destroy millions of innocent lives. It also revealed uncomfortable truths about the human capacity for evil. To take a stand against that evil, world leaders realized that a truly international approach was needed.

Even before the war was over, representatives from fifty nations gathered in San Francisco. Their goal was to create a truly international organization, dedicated to world peace and human rights. On October 24, 1945, the delegates approved the charter, or founding document, of the United Nations. The United States, Great Britain, and the Soviet Union—the Allies who had fought together to defeat Nazi Germany—were among the first to sign it.

The Universal Declaration of Human Rights

One of the first and most important actions of the United Nations was to confront the human rights issues raised by the war. The result was the Universal Declaration of Human Rights, adopted by the General Assembly of the United Nations on December 10, 1948.

Though it owed much to earlier codes, it was unique in its international scope. The General Assembly of the United Nations declared it to be "a common standard of achievement for all peoples and all nations." The first two articles set the tone for the twenty-eight that would follow.

Article 1 proclaimed:

All human beings are born free and equal in dignity and rights. They are endowed with reason and conscience and should act towards one another in a spirit of brotherhood.[7]

Article 2 made clear that no human being should be denied these rights:

> Everyone is entitled to all the rights and freedoms set forth in this Declaration, without distinction of any kind, such as race, colour, sex, language, religion, political or other opinion, national or social origin, property, birth or other status.[8]

Unfortunately, putting the Articles of the Declaration into practice proved to be more difficult than writing them. Nations continued to violate the rights of their own citizens. Armies continued to commit atrocities in war.

Still, human rights advocates believe that the Declaration is worthwhile. It sets a standard by which societies and individuals may be judged. Perhaps more importantly, its vision of a just and equitable world provides a worthy goal for the future of humankind.

6

Human Rights and Civil Disobedience

In the hands of human rights activists with the courage of their convictions, civil disobedience is a powerful tool. In the mid-twentieth century, Mohandas K. Gandhi used it to free India from British rule. Martin Luther King, Jr., used it to oppose racial segregation in the American South.

Though Gandhi and King came from very different cultures, they had much in common. Both found inspiration and practical guidance in Henry David Thoreau's landmark essay on civil disobedience. Both used this nonviolent

60

strategy to secure the rights of people of color in a white-dominated society. Both dedicated their lives to the cause of freedom, and both died at the hands of assassins. They became towering figures in modern history—men of peace who challenged old prejudices and sought a better way of life for oppressed people.

Public Law and Private Morality

Henry David Thoreau stood out from his own era as Gandhi and King stood out from theirs. Before he put his ideas on civil disobedience into words, he put them into practice. In 1846, the United States began what Thoreau considered an unjust war against Mexico. In addition, slavery remained an ever-present reminder that in America, freedom was not for everyone.

In protest, Thoreau refused to pay his poll tax and was arrested. He spent a night in jail before an aunt came forward and paid the tax

The philosopher Henry David Thoreau (1817–1862) was an American whose writings and actions inspired nonviolent movements for change all over the world.

for him. This brief imprisonment made a powerful statement, which Thoreau later discussed in "Civil Disobedience." He began with the idea that morality is more important than legality:

> Must a citizen . . . resign his conscience to the legislator? Why has every man a conscience, then? I think that we should be men first, and subjects afterward. It is not desirable to cultivate a respect for the law, so much as for the right.[1]

In addition to breaking unjust laws, human rights activists have often challenged unfair social policies or business practices. Their methods are nonviolent and may include a variety of marches, rallies, and demonstrations. Instead of fighting back when force is used against them, activists meet that force with passive resistance. In every case, the goal is to dramatize injustice in as public a manner as possible.

In the long crusade against racial segregation in the South, activists began by breaking laws that separated people by race. For example, they staged sit-ins at whites-only lunch counters, lined up to drink at whites-only water fountains, and refused to sit in the rear "colored" section of city buses. Hundreds went to jail for these actions, and yet the protests did not stop.

The "Great Soul" of India

The same kind of dedication to principle marked the long struggle for India's independence from Great Britain. As leader of the movement, Mohandas K. Gandhi was firmly committed to nonviolence. To him, it was more than a tactic for achieving social change. It was a way of life.

Gandhi was strongly influenced by the work of Henry David Thoreau. Reading "Civil Disobedience" was a revelation for him. He called it "a masterly treatise" which "left a deep impression on me."[2]

In his early experiments with nonviolent social protest, Gandhi used the term "passive resistance." He soon became dissatisfied with it. He noted,

> In a meeting of Europeans I found that the term "passive resistance" was too narrowly construed, that it was supposed to be a weapon of the weak, that it could be characterized by hatred, and that it could finally [show] itself as violence.[3]

He put out a call for suggestions for a new word to describe the Indian struggle. The eventual result was *satyagraha*, which combines "truth" and "firmness." This implies that resistance to evil and injustice is active rather than passive. Nonviolence and passivity are not the same thing.

Gandhi believed in vigorous action, but without violence. For example, he once led a protest against the British salt tax in India. He did this by marching to the ocean and making salt illegally. He then encouraged the equally illegal sale of untaxed salt all over India.

It was activities such as this that earned him the title *mahatma*, meaning "great soul." In time, that term would all but replace his given name.

Gandhi's Crusades for Human Rights

Gandhi's special gift was his ability to use spiritual methods to achieve political goals, using his moral authority to oppose many forms of injustice. He not only took on the British Empire in the cause of political freedom, he also challenged the Hindu caste system in the cause of human equality.

Caste in the Hindu religion was a hereditary structure of social classes. The caste into which a person was born determined his or her worth as a human being. The ancient religious texts known as the Vedas established four castes. They ranged from the Brahmans, or priests, to the Sudras, or workers and servants.

Somewhere along the way, a fifth group emerged: a permanent underclass known as "Untouchables." Gandhi called them "Harijans," or "children of God." He opposed the whole caste system because he believed in the equality of all people, but it was the plight of the Harijans that attracted his special attention and compassion.

The word "untouchable" was not used in a symbolic sense. Orthodox, or strictly observant, Hindus were literally forbidden to touch a Harijan in any way. Even objects that an Untouchable handled became "unclean."

Untouchables belonged nowhere. They could not even enter a Hindu temple to worship. As Louis Fischer explained:

[Untouchables] inhabit the worst sections of the world's worst urban slums, and in villages they live on the lowest outskirts into which the filth and dirty waters drain, but it is the only water that they can use, for the well is forbidden to them. It would be polluted.[4]

In other words, just the touch of a Harijan would "pollute" the entire well and make its water unusable for others.

Mohandas K. Gandhi, known as "Mahatma," or "Great Soul," used spiritual methods to achieve political goals of independence for India and rights for Untouchables. He is shown here with Margaret Sanger, the American family planning pioneer.

Gandhi was as determined to secure the rights of Untouchables as he was to win India's freedom from British rule. In 1920, he convinced the Indian National Congress to pass a resolution calling for the end of untouchability.

That resolution had little effect on the larger society, even though it was sponsored by the much-admired Gandhi. Untouchability was deeply entrenched in Indian life. Not until 1950 would it be outlawed, and even then prejudice against Harijans would linger.

Gandhi had more success winning India's freedom from the British. Under his leadership, growing numbers of Indians simply refused to cooperate with the government in any way. Even for the mighty British Empire, maintaining control in a country that did not want it simply became too time-consuming and expensive. On August 15, 1947, Britain bowed to the inevitable; India became a free and sovereign nation.

Gandhi's long struggle became a shining example of what could be accomplished through nonviolent resistance. In the United States, a young African-American clergyman saw in that example a way to fight racial segregation in the South.

The Struggle Against Racial Segregation in America

Martin Luther King, Jr., was a seminary student when he became aware of Gandhi's philosophy of nonviolence. At the time, King was on what he described as "a serious intellectual quest for a method to eliminate social evil."[5] He found it unexpectedly, in a sermon by Dr. Mordecai Johnson, president of Howard University:

> Dr. Johnson had just returned from a trip to India, and, to my great interest, he spoke of the life and teachings of Mahatma Gandhi. His message was so profound and electrifying that I left the meeting and bought a half-dozen books on Gandhi's life and works.[6]

Reading about Gandhi reminded King of his undergraduate days, when he had read Henry David Thoreau's essay on civil disobedience. "I was so deeply moved that I reread the work several times," he wrote.[7] Meeting these ideas again in the work of a man who lived on the other side of the world was a thrilling experience: "I came to feel that this was the only morally and practically sound method open to oppressed people in their struggle for freedom."[8]

The Reverend Martin Luther King, Jr., first came to national prominence during the bus boycott in Montgomery, Alabama. On December 1, 1955, an African-American seamstress was seated in the back "colored section" of a crowded city bus. A white man boarded and found no empty seats, so he ordered the woman to move. By law, that was his right.

Seamstress Rosa Parks knew the law as well as anyone, but this time she refused to obey it. She was promptly arrested. The African-American community of Montgomery was outraged. They were accustomed to arrests for minor infractions, but somehow this one became the proverbial last straw. They were ready to take action.

Martin Luther King sensed that the time was right. Within five days, he and his fellow activists had organized a boycott against Montgomery's bus system. It began on December 5.

That morning, King and his wife, Coretta, were nervous. They had feverishly spread the word through the African-American community, but they had no way of knowing what kind of response they would get. The first bus of the day was scheduled to pass their house at six o'clock. On a normal weekday it would be filled with African-American people going to work.

On this day, it was empty. The Kings were jubilant. They watched the next bus and the next. Aside from two white passengers, those buses were also empty.

The promise of that Monday morning in Montgomery was not realized for more than a year. During that time the protesters held rallies to keep up morale. They organized car pools to take people back and forth to work. They faced violence, hatred, and harassment. Finally, on December 21, 1956, racial segregation on the buses of Montgomery came to an official end.

Martin Luther King, Jr., and those who worked with him knew that this ending was in fact the beginning of a much larger struggle for true equality. It would be long and it would be hard. Some people would grow impatient with nonviolence and want to fight back.

Dr. Martin Luther King, Jr., a Baptist minister, used nonviolent civil disobedience to achieve rights for African Americans.

For them, King echoed the message of Gandhi and Thoreau: that nonviolent resistance *is* fighting back. Like Gandhi, King was not happy with the phrase "passive resistance." He believed that it gave

> the false impression that . . . the resister quietly and passively accepts evil. But nothing is further from the truth. . . . The method is passive physically, but strongly active spiritually. It is not passive nonresistance to evil, it is active nonviolent resistance to evil.[9]

The "active nonviolent resistance" that won the day in Montgomery would be severely tested when it faced the racism and bigotry that created those laws in the first place. That struggle would continue into the 1960s and beyond.

7

The Activist
Sixties

The 1960s will always be remembered as a time of social upheaval and change in the United States. Minority groups demanded equal rights and poor people sought a way out of their poverty. Young people dared to believe that a generation committed to social justice could make a difference in the world. Some actually thought they could save it.

Though the activism of the sixties fell short of saving the world, it did produce important gains for human rights. African Americans moved closer to true social equality. The most ambitious antipoverty

program in American history began. The Supreme
Court created new legal safeguards for individual
rights.

Internationally, the United Nations General
Assembly formally condemned South Africa's policy
of apartheid, or racial separatism. This 1961 resolution was part of a long and painful struggle that
would last into the 1990s. There were also human
rights activities in the Communist world, most
notably "Prague Spring" in Czechoslovakia and the
daring humanitarian work of physicist Andrei
Sakharov in the Soviet Union.

Americans on the March

In the United States, the African-American civil
rights movement blazed a trail of activism that others would follow. By the end of the 1950s,
African-American activists had learned that changing
the law was not enough. Somebody had to take the
risk of putting those changes into practice. African-
American students had to enroll in previously
all-white schools. African-American customers had to
sit down at "white" lunch counters and wait to be
served. African-American voters had to register and
then go to the polls on election day.

In 1960, activist Ella Baker and others formed
the Student Nonviolent Coordinating Committee
(SNCC) to promote this kind of direct action.
Sympathetic whites joined the effort. Within two
months of its founding, SNCC had organized lunch
counter sit-ins in fifty-four cities.

The crusade for racial equality captured the imagination of many young people. In 1962, sixty idealistic college students met at Port Huron, Michigan, to found an organization and create a manifesto, or statement of principles. The group known as Students for a Democratic Society (SDS) grew out of that meeting.

By the end of its first year, the SDS had grown from sixty members to over eight thousand. Its members were deeply involved in the African-American civil rights movement. Many were on hand for one of the true milestones of the sixties: the March on Washington for Jobs and Freedom.

"I Have a Dream"

On August 28, 1963, a quarter of a million people assembled at the Lincoln Memorial. Nearly a third of them were white. They had come to support the aspirations of African-American people and the cause of human rights. On that sticky-hot summer day, Martin Luther King, Jr., first delivered the speech that was to become one of the most memorable orations in American history:

"I have a dream," he said, "that one day on the red hills of Georgia the sons of former slaves and the sons of former slaveowners will be able to sit down together at the table of brotherhood. . . ."[1]

"The Movement," as it became known, gathered momentum after the march on Washington. SDS activist Todd Gitlin wrote about the importance of that time in his book on the sixties:

Vivid days like August 28, 1963, become watersheds. The next day, everyone agrees that time has parted into time before and time after. The conflicts come in the interpretation. What has become possible and impossible now? What else is to be done?[2]

The Battle in Berkeley

To students at the University of California in Berkeley, the "what else" was the free speech movement. It began almost by accident in 1964, when the university prohibited political activity in a popular gathering spot on campus.

Students protested what they believed to be a violation of their rights. When the university ignored them, they "moved from demanding a change in the new rule to a critique of the entire structure of the university and of an education geared to preparing graduates for white-collar corporate jobs," according to one historian.[3]

By tapping into the discontents of youth, the Berkeley free speech movement helped to create a counterculture. It was a massive rebellion against the getting-and-spending, workaday culture of middle-class America. There had to be more to life than that, young people said, and they set out to find it. The most radical of them became known as hippies.

There was no organization to join to become a hippie; no creed or manifesto to accept; no oath to swear. Though most hippies came from privileged middle-class backgrounds, they identified with the poor and the oppressed. In the process, they helped to inspire social protest by disadvantaged minorities.

Other People, Other Dreams

Among those minorities who pressed for their rights were American Indians and Mexican Americans. Both were people of color in an overwhelmingly white society. Both had been exploited by that society and had endured prejudice and discrimination at its hands. In the ferment of the sixties, both saw an opportunity to correct old injustices.

The Mexican-American movement of the early and mid-sixties centered on the plight of migrant farm workers. These people were the poorest of the poor. They lived a hand-to-mouth existence, following the crops. Whole families would work from dawn to sundown. Many of them earned just enough for food and a day's rent on a ramshackle cabin without utilities.

In 1962, Cesar Estrada Chavez began forming the organization that would eventually be called the United Farm Workers of America (UFW). In 1965, with a tiny membership and almost no money, the fledgling union began a strike against California grape growers.

The following year, Chavez followed the lead of Martin Luther King and Mohandas K. Gandhi. He organized a march from the California farm town of Delano to the state capital in Sacramento, 245 miles away. The pilgrimage, which lasted twenty-five days, focused nationwide attention on farm worker issues. By the time it ended, the union had its first labor contract. This agreement between the growers and the union established higher wages, fairer hiring practices, and better working conditions.

The American Indian Movement (AIM) chose an equally dramatic way to arouse public opinion. In November 1969, seventy-eight young activists landed on Alcatraz Island in San Francisco Bay. They claimed it "in the name of all American Indians."[4]

The activists were responding to generations of mistreatment. From the time Europeans first arrived in what was to them the "New World," they killed native peoples and displaced them from their lands. The government made treaties and broke them, finally shuttling the native tribes onto reservations. On most of these reservations, poverty and hopelessness are daily realities of life.

AIM sought to right these wrongs. The activists based their claims on an 1868 treaty with the Sioux nation. It stated that the Indians could claim any federal land "which is not mineral land, nor reserved by the United States for special purposes other than Indian occupation."[5]

Alcatraz, deserted since the 1963 close of the federal prison of the same name, fit the specifications of the treaty perfectly. At least the AIM members thought so. The government did not agree, claiming that the island was still under federal control. After nearly two years of occupation, federal marshals removed the protesters.

Building the Great Society

Protests like the American Indian occupation of Alcatraz did not magically transform society, abolish poverty, or end racial and ethnic discrimination. However, the climate of change that spawned those movements convinced the government that something had to be done to help disadvantaged minorities.

President Lyndon B. Johnson responded with the War on Poverty: "Because it is right, because it is wise, and because, for the first time in our history, it is possible to conquer poverty."[6]

The War on Poverty was an attempt to attack the problems of poverty from many directions. Shown is a group of welfare recipients waiting at the Illinois capitol building in 1968 to express their views.

War on Poverty programs attacked the problem from many different directions. Unemployment insurance, which provided temporary income for people who lost their jobs, was improved. The food stamp program, which provided coupons for the purchase of food, was expanded so more poor people could qualify.

Legislation created the Job Corps to expand employment opportunities for young people and Head Start preschools for underprivileged toddlers. Volunteers In Service To America (VISTA) recruited people from all walks of life to work within impoverished communities. For example, one VISTA volunteer went to Utah to help establish a daycare center for the children of Navajo farm workers. Another went to Virginia to work in a shelter for abused women.

In addition to the direct, hands-on way of helping the poor, a variety of other projects addressed the problem of poverty. President Johnson said:

> We are fully aware that this program will not eliminate all the poverty in America in a few months or a few years. Poverty is deeply rooted and its causes are many. But this program will show the way to new opportunities for millions of our fellow citizens.[7]

The War on Poverty was part of Johnson's vision of a "Great Society." Its goal was to bring "an end to poverty and racial injustice" and produce "abundance and liberty for all."[8] The program was well timed and generally effective. It made a difference in the lives of many people. It might have made an even greater difference if not for United States' involvement in a deadlier kind of war.

An Unrighteous War

For almost a hundred years, the Southeast Asian nation of Vietnam was a colony of France. In the 1950s, the country united against French occupation and gained independence. However, the unity did not last. Because of internal disputes, Vietnam was divided into the Communist North and the non-Communist South.

The Soviet Union and China backed the North. The United States and other Western democracies backed the South.

At first, American involvement in Vietnam was limited to financial support, weapons, and about sixteen thousand "military advisors," who were there to help the South Vietnamese plan the defense of their homeland.

Over time, American involvement in Vietnam escalated, or grew. In August 1964, American planes began bombarding North Vietnam. Ground troops followed: over two hundred thousand in 1965 and another two hundred thousand in 1966. By early 1968, there were half a million American soldiers in Vietnam, and the Air Force was dropping thousands of tons of bombs on the North.

The war in Vietnam became the central issue of the late 1960s. Activist groups in the United States and even in Europe united against it. Young men burned their draft cards in public ceremonies. Some fled to Canada to avoid being forced to serve in a war they believed to be immoral.

Some protesters opposed all war as a matter of principle. Others focused on Vietnam, on the grounds that the United States had no right to interfere in the internal disputes of another country.

Throughout the counterculture, buttons and banners and T-shirts bore slogans such as WAR IS UNHEALTHY FOR CHILDREN AND OTHER LIVING THINGS and SUPPOSE THEY GAVE A WAR AND NOBODY CAME. War came to be considered the ultimate violation of

Not all of those opposed to the Vietnam War were young students. Shown are people making the peace sign at an antiwar demonstration in Chicago in 1968.

human rights, turning some people into killers and others into victims.

The war in Vietnam brought down the Johnson presidency. In 1968, feeling against Johnson ran so high that he decided not to seek another term. This decision turned the 1968 Democratic National Convention into a political free-for-all.

When delegates gathered in Chicago to choose a candidate, they were outnumbered by protesters. Thousands of activists, led by the politically aware SDS, disrupted the convention and confronted police in the streets. They wanted an antiwar candidate, like Senator Eugene McCarthy or Senator George McGovern. Instead, they got Hubert H. Humphrey, Johnson's vice president and a supporter of U.S. policy in Vietnam.

The controversy surrounding Humphrey's candidacy put Republican Richard Nixon in the White House. It also caused changes within the student movement.

The Women's Movement

After the 1968 presidential election, activists who had focused almost entirely on Vietnam began turning their attention to other issues, such as women's rights.

It was an issue whose time had come. Until 1920, American women did not have the right to vote. They lived their entire lives under the control of men. As children, they were supposed to be obedient to their fathers; as adults, to their husbands. Their worth as human beings was determined by their role as wives, mothers, and homemakers.

The women's movement of the 1970s dealt with a variety of social and economic issues affecting women, from rape and domestic violence to equal rights in the workplace. Its most controversial and enduring issue was abortion. On January 22, 1973, the United States Supreme Court affirmed a woman's right to end an unwanted pregnancy in the landmark case of *Roe* v. *Wade.*

Abortion was no longer a crime, but many people remained convinced that it was a sin. Abortion, they

The women's movement of the 1960s grew out of the earlier movement for women's suffrage, or voting rights. Shown is a suffrage parade in New York City in 1912. Despite decades of effort, women did not gain the right to vote until 1920.

claimed, was nothing less than murder. Thus began a debate that has continued into the twenty-first century and become a major human rights issue for people on both sides.

Human Rights in the Communist World

Sixties activism was not limited to the United States, or even to the free world. In the Soviet Union and its republics, there were brave people who dared to stand against the human rights abuses of their own governments.

In Prague, Czechoslovakia, a movement known as "Prague Spring" challenged the oppressive practices of the government. In 1968, Prague Spring activists called for human rights reforms and the "democratization" of the country's political and economic system. The goal was an ambitious one: to create a "unique experiment in democratic communism."[9]

The reform program was enormously popular in Czechoslovakia, but hard-line Communists outside the country considered it dangerous. On August 20, half a million troops from the Soviet Union, Poland, Hungary, Bulgaria, and East Germany invaded Czechoslovakia.

The reform leaders were arrested and forced to renounce most of their program. Thus, the Czech experiment in democratic communism came to an end less than six months after it began. Its influence, however, may not have ended. Radio Free Europe pointed out that Prague Spring's reforms "are often seen as . . . forerunners to Mikhail Gorbachev's reform policies . . . in the 1980s in the USSR."[10]

An even more powerful influence on Soviet reform was Andrei Sakharov, whose 1968 essay "Reflection on Progress, Coexistence and Intellectual Freedom" launched a new Soviet human rights movement. Sakharov was a brilliant physicist who developed the Soviet hydrogen bomb, then devoted himself to exposing its horrors. He worked for a ban on test explosions that would release deadly radiation into the air, and he spoke out on the dangers of nuclear warfare. Over the years he became interested in human rights and political issues.

For his work on behalf of justice, Sakharov was persecuted in his own country. His honors in the rest of the world included the Nobel Peace Prize of 1975. The Nobel committee called him "the conscience of mankind" and praised him for fighting "not only against the abuse of power and violations of human dignity . . . [but] for the ideal of a state founded on the principle of justice for all."[11]

Andrei Sakharov and other activists of the sixties were not able to solve all the problems of human-kind. Still, their work transformed that boisterous decade into a time when people came together and tried to make a difference in the world. This was their legacy to those who would continue the struggle for human rights into the twenty-first century.

8

The New Internationalism

The human rights movement became truly international in scope during the last quarter of the twentieth century. In an age of rapid transportation and nearly instantaneous communication, abuses anywhere affected people everywhere. Governments, human rights organizations, and concerned individuals began to realize that responsibility for human rights did not stop at national borders.

In spite of this growing conviction, abusive governments continued to hide behind national sovereignty, the right of a nation to conduct its own affairs. Their claim was simple—so long as a government's actions affected only its own citizens, they believed outsiders had no right to interfere.

Human Rights Goes Global

The globalization of human rights began in earnest in the 1970s. The growth of nongovernmental organizations (NGOs) was a major factor in this new international perspective. NGOs are private groups; most of them are operated as nonprofit charities, funded by donations. Though they may have paid staff, many NGOs also use a large number of volunteer workers.

The oldest and perhaps best known of the major human rights NGOs is Amnesty International. It was founded in 1960 by British attorney Peter Benenson. Amnesty took on the cause of "prisoners of conscience"—people imprisoned because they opposed various policies of their governments. Local chapters would "adopt" a particular prisoner and flood his or her government with letters protesting the injustice and demanding the prisoner's release.

By the mid-1970s, Amnesty had become the world's largest human rights organization, winning the Nobel Peace Prize in 1977. It expanded its scope to include torture cases and took a stand against the death penalty. It also began a general public education program on human rights and lobbied governments on human rights issues.

Another important NGO is Human Rights Watch, which was formed by the merger of several smaller human rights groups. This NGO documents human rights abuses all over the world, publicizes those abuses, and fights for social and political reform.

In every part of the world there have always been "hot spots," where human rights were routinely violated. For example, in Southeast Asia, a brutal regime turned all of Cambodia into a prison camp. In South America, the government of Argentina used terrorism and murder as political tools. In South Africa, a tiny minority of whites stripped the black majority of its rights. These violations sharpened the international conflicts over human rights.

The Helsinki Accords

Not all the multinational efforts on behalf of human rights were the work of NGOs or the United Nations. One important, though not legally binding, agreement came out of a major conference between the Soviet and Western powers.

On August 1, 1975, in Helsinki, Finland, representatives from thirty-five nations signed a document that became known as the Helsinki Accords. Most delegates came from the North Atlantic Treaty Organization (NATO), headed by the United States and Great Britain, and the Warsaw Pact nations, headed by the Soviet Union.

The Helsinki Accords linked peace and national security to human rights in a bold new way. The Soviets wanted guarantees of national borders, especially in Eastern Europe. Their goal was to protect the territorial gains they had made in World War II.

NATO wanted free exchange of ideas and greater freedom of travel across those borders. It also wanted greater respect for human rights in Soviet bloc nations.

Both got what they wanted—at least on paper. Because the agreement was not legally binding, there was no provision for enforcement. In the years to come, its principles would be violated many times. Still, the Helsinki Accords set a standard by which people could judge one another's behavior.

The agreement did not stop with nations. It also called upon private individuals to help implement human rights reforms in their counties. Many activists regard this as the striking feature of the Helsinki Accords; for the first time in history, an international document had declared human rights to be everybody's business.

Human Rights and U.S. Foreign Policy

After the Helsinki Accords, human rights played an increasingly important role in the foreign policy of the United States. In 1976, Congress added an amendment to the Foreign Assistance Act of 1961. The new Section 502B tied U.S. foreign aid to a country's human rights practices. It clearly stated that "a principal goal of the foreign policy of the United States is to promote the increased observance of internationally recognized human rights by all countries."

To accomplish this, Congress banned security assistance to any country that "engages in a consistent pattern of gross violations of internationally recognized human rights."[1] There were loopholes, or carefully worded exceptions, in this law. Still, the attempt to tie political and economic support to human rights practices was a meaningful accomplishment.

When President Jimmy Carter took office in 1977, he made this focus on human rights an important part of his foreign policy. During his four years in office, Carter accomplished many things. He

President Jimmy Carter, elected in 1976, made the struggle for human rights an important part of his foreign policy. He is shown here with Martin Luther King, Sr., father of the slain civil rights leader.

established the post of Assistant Secretary of State for Human Rights, directed the State Department to monitor and report on human rights practices in various countries, and cut off military aid to repressive governments.

Like other American leaders, Carter feared the spread of communism. This sometimes made repressive, but anti-Communist, regimes seem like the lesser of two evils. Ignoring the human rights abuses of "friendly" dictators was a political decision.

The Khmer Rouge of Cambodia

During the Vietnam War, Cambodian premier Lon Nol was one of these pro-American dictators. He ruled by decree, assassinated or imprisoned his enemies, and murdered and terrorized his own people. Still, the United States backed his regime against a pro-Communist force known as the Khmer Rouge, which was even more brutal than Lon Nol. The U.S. Air Force bombed Cambodia with "three times as many tons of conventional explosives as fell on Japan in all of World War II."[2]

Even this did not stop the Khmer Rouge. On April 17, 1975, they took the capital city of Phnom Penh. Their first victims were Cambodians known to have supported the Lon Nol government or the United States. Next came educated people such as teachers and doctors, and anyone judged to be "contaminated" by Western influences.

People were driven from the cities and made to work on collective farms. There, millions starved or were executed for minor offenses against the regime. Human rights ceased to exist.

Survivor Dith Pran later spoke of "killing grounds with bones and skulls everywhere among the trees and wells. . . . You could always tell the killing grounds because the grass grew taller and greener where the bodies were buried."[3]

The Khmer Rouge ruled Cambodia for four and a half years. In that time, they killed at least 2 million of the country's 7 million people.

"The Disappeared" of Argentina

Half a world away in Argentina, a military coup overthrew the government of President Isabel Martinez de Peron. On March 24, 1976, the horror that became known as the "dirty war" began. Liberals, leftists, and anyone suspected of collaboration with the previous government were grabbed off the streets.

These people were not formally arrested, charged with specific crimes, or brought to trial. They simply "disappeared." The authorities denied knowledge of their fate to anyone who inquired. They became *Los Desaparecidos*—"The Disappeared."

Journalists and human rights activists investigated the disappearances and found disturbing evidence that Los Desaparecidos were in fact tortured, starved, and usually killed. According to Argentine journalist Jacobo Timerman:

> Entire families disappeared. The bodies were covered with cement and thrown to the

bottom of the river. . . . [They] were thrown into old cemeteries under existing graves. Never to be found. [They] were heaved into the middle of the sea from helicopters.[4]

The dirty war lasted until 1983. In that time, thousands died anonymous deaths because of their actual or suspected political beliefs. An entire population was terrorized and stripped of fundamental rights.

Apartheid in South Africa

Argentina was not the only country where people disappeared without trace; it happened in South Africa as well. Anyone who challenged the policy of strict racial separatism known as apartheid was apt to run afoul of the government. Many of these people simply vanished and were never heard from again. Others were jailed. Under South African law, people could be imprisoned without charges or trial for an indefinite period of time.

In a country where 85 percent of the population was black, Asian, or of mixed race, a tiny white minority kept an iron grip on power. Over time, a series of increasingly repressive race laws stripped black South Africans of all rights. They could not even enter white cities and townships except to work.

In 1960, a young black activist named Nelson Mandela publicly committed an act of civil disobedience by burning his passbook (identity papers the government required black people to carry). He did it to dramatize the injustice of South Africa's apartheid laws and to serve the cause of black freedom. He had no idea he would be serving that cause as a prisoner of conscience.

Less than three years later, Nelson Mandela was sentenced to life in prison. He was found guilty of plotting "the commission of acts of violence and destruction throughout the country" in order to "bring about in the Republic of South Africa chaos, disorder and turmoil."[5]

Nelson Mandela was to remain in prison for twenty-seven years. In that time he became the world's most famous prisoner and the "patron saint" of black liberation in South Africa.

An Outcast Among Nations

By the late 1970s, apartheid had become an international issue. In 1977, the United Nations met in general council to order an arms embargo against the Republic of South Africa. In 1980, a UN committee called for strengthening the embargo. Prohibiting the sale of arms to South Africa was not enough. The committee wanted sanctions against "the export to South Africa of dual-purpose items . . . with the potential for . . . military use."[6] These included such things as aircraft parts, electronic equipment, and computers.

Six years after the United Nations embargo, the United States imposed its own economic and political sanctions. In 1986, Congress overrode a veto by President Ronald Reagan to prohibit American

Nelson Mandela, shown here with President Bill Clinton, was imprisoned for twenty-seven years because of his resistance to apartheid. Mandela became the first black president of South Africa in 1994.

companies and individuals from doing business with South Africa. This action was helped along by human rights activists who pressured American universities and other institutions to take their investments out of the South African stock market.

Historians and other experts disagree on the influence of United States and United Nations sanctions. Many feel that the effect was more symbolic than actual. Still, sanctions were part of the pressure on the white South African government. By 1990, that pressure had begun to produce real change.

Nelson Mandela was released from prison on February 11, 1990. Not only did he emerge a hero to black South Africans, he impressed many whites with his moderate stance. He called for a South Africa that would belong to all its citizens, regardless of race. In 1993, he was awarded the Nobel Peace Prize for his work in promoting human rights and racial justice in his homeland.

In 1994, Nelson Mandela became president of South Africa after the free and open election he had wanted for so many years. In 1996, his government established the Truth and Reconciliation Commission. This agency was charged with investigating atrocities and finding out who was responsible for them. Mandela wanted to be sure all the facts were revealed and that innocent people were not held accountable for crimes they did not commit. He believed that justice rather than revenge would allow South Africa to begin the long process of healing.

A Place Called Tiananmen Square

While South Africa struggled with apartheid, the People's Republic of China also experienced a burst of human rights activism. It came mostly from university students, who wanted a more open and free society than the government would allow.

The movement began in the mid-1980s. China was experiencing economic problems and widespread political corruption, or dishonesty and cheating in government. Young people began to lose faith in communism as practiced in China and to desire democratic reforms. Their efforts to bring about these reforms led to conflict with the government and in time, to the tragedy of Tiananmen Square.

In the long history of China, June 4, 1989, will stand as a landmark date. After days of rioting and bloodshed, the capital city of Beijing was under martial law, or military control. Thousands of students and supporters massed in Tiananmen Square. Other protests flared up around the country.

The authorities feared that the mounting rebellion would turn into a full-scale revolution. On the evening of June 3, Martial Law Command was ordered to clear Tiananmen Square. The operation was supposed to be peaceful. Unfortunately, it did not turn out that way.

A Fateful Night

Students and their supporters tried to keep the troops from ever reaching the square. They even set up roadblocks. At Muxidi Bridge, troops tried to

In 1989, Tiananmen Square in Beijing, China, was the site of massive demonstrations by those who wanted political reforms. It is estimated that as many as five thousand people died in the clash between protesters and government forces.

clear the way by throwing canisters of tear gas and firing rubber bullets. When that failed, they opened fire. The protesters panicked and tried to retreat, but they were hindered by their own roadblocks. Many were shot or trampled in the confusion. This scene was repeated at other sites throughout the city.

The exact casualty figures are unknown. CNN estimated that as many as five thousand people may have died at Tiananmen.[7] The Chinese government gave a much lower figure—241 killed and about seven thousand wounded.[8]

By 1:00 A.M. on June 4, the troops had passed the

roadblocks and were massing at Tiananmen Square. They used loudspeakers to order the crowd to leave. Many did leave, but others held their ground.

At 4:00 A.M., the lights in the square went out. When they came back on, the students found themselves surrounded by armed soldiers. According to a State Security Ministry report, "Tension gripped the protestors, especially when they saw rows of tanks and armored cars moving slowly through the Square from its north edge."[9]

The students retreated. By 5:40 A.M., Tiananmen Square had been cleared. The protest was over. Afterwards, according to *Tiananmen Papers* editor Andrew J. Nathan, "China seemed shrouded in a dour mist that harbored a spiritual emptiness. . . . Something had died."[10]

International response to Tiananmen was swift. The World Bank put a freeze on loans to China. The United States and a dozen other countries imposed various kinds of political and economic sanctions.

World reactions to China, as well as to South Africa, signaled the beginning of a new worldwide emphasis on human rights. This emerging movement would soon face its greatest test: finding a way to balance the rights of human beings with the sovereignty of national governments.

9

Unfinished Business

The last years of the twentieth century brought momentous political changes that had a lasting impact on human rights. The most stunning of these was the breakup of the Soviet Union in 1991. Though the collapse raised new hopes for freedom, it also led to confusion and ethnic violence. These in turn led to serious human rights abuses.

Abuses were not limited to the former Soviet Union. In the late twentieth century and into the twenty-first, there were ethnic and racial conflict, terrorism, and violent oppression in many parts of the world. In addition, technological advances and changing ideas about the scope of human rights raised new issues and gave new importance to older ones.

To better deal with these issues, the United Nations established the post of High Commissioner for Human Rights in 1993. Unlike the already-existing UN Commission on Human Rights, the office of the commissioner is a permanent, full-time agency of the United Nations. This signaled the beginning of a new era. The world community was coming to realize that only an international agency with power to act could stem the tide of abuse.

Ethnic Warfare in Bosnia-Herzegovina

After the breakup of the Soviet Union, many of the Communist satellite countries in Eastern Europe became independent nation-states. Many of them were not prepared for self-government. The result was political and economic instability. In Bosnia-Herzegovina, that instability led to bloody ethnic warfare. This small republic had once been part of Yugoslavia, which had in turn been an autonomous, or self-governing, Communist republic. In the early 1990s, Yugoslavia splintered into a disorganized collection of tiny republics.

By 1991, three competing ethnic groups in Bosnia-Herzegovina were trying to destroy each other. Croats, Serbs, and Muslims became locked in a bloody war that lasted for three years. Terrorism and atrocities against civilians became the norm in that hate-torn land.

Zlata Filipović was eleven years old when war came to her home city of Sarajevo. Her wartime diary touched readers all over the world. It was a child's account of living in constant fear, hiding in basements to escape constant shelling, and going hungry because the attackers cut off food supplies to the besieged city.

Zlata did not understand the ethnic hatred that lay behind the brutality. She wrote in her diary:

> I keep wanting to explain these stupid politics to myself, because it seems to me that politics caused this war, making it our everyday reality. . . . It looks to me as though these politics mean Serbs, Croats and Muslims. But they are all people. They are all the same. They all look like people, there's no difference. . . . Now politics has started meddling around. It has put an "S" on Serbs, an "M"' on Muslims and a "C" on Croats, it wants to separate them.[1]

The war lasted for more than three years before the international community took action. In that time, the term "ethnic cleansing" came into use to describe what was happening. It is the systematic and forcible removal of a particular group from an area. The aim is to create "ethnically pure" regions. The methods range from forced migrations to mass murder.

For example, in August 1992, Bosnian Serbs rounded up the entire Muslim population of Sanski Most, a town in northern Bosnia. About fifteen hundred people were forced to leave their homes, taking only what they could carry. The journey began in buses and cars. It ended on foot, as men, women, and children were marched at gunpoint along a narrow mountain road. The road was cratered by artillery shelling. Mines, or buried explosive devices, lined one side.

In order to get to their destination, the deportees had to cross what investigative journalist Maud S. Beelman described as "a high wall of boulders dynamited from the mountainside." Beelman wrote:

> A crippled man was carried over, his wheelchair passed after him. Babies were handed to their mothers. Old men and women, stooped with age, struggled over the rocks. . . . The foot journey lasted six hours and covered twelve miles.[2]

Bloodshed in Rwanda

During the Bosnian war, another deadly situation developed in the small African nation of Rwanda. Years of ethnic tension between the Hutu and Tutsi tribes had grown out of the fact that the Tutsi, though accounting for only 20 percent of the population, held most of the wealth and power. The majority Hutus were mostly poor farmers.

On April 6, 1994, a plane carrying president Juvenal Habyarimana, a Hutu, was shot down, killing everyone on board. The attack was probably carried out by extremists within Habyarimana's own government who disagreed with some of his policies. Still, it triggered a murderous rampage by Hutus against the hated Tutsi minority.

According to the Department of Peace Studies at Great Britain's Bradford University, as many as eight hundred thousand men, women, and children were killed within a three-month period. Tens of thousands more "were physically and psychologically afflicted for life through maiming, rape and other trauma; over two million fled to neighboring countries and maybe [one million] became internally displaced within Rwanda."[3]

Neither the United Nations nor any other international body would take military action to stop the slaughter. As in Bosnia, the UN resisted direct interference in the internal affairs of a sovereign nation. The Committee of the Joint Evaluation of Emergency Assistance to Rwanda considered "the inactivity of the UN" to be "tragic."[4] Human Rights Watch stated that "the international community shamefully turned its back on genocide in Rwanda."[5]

An Invitation to East Timor

By 1999, the international community had grown bolder in defense of human rights. When death squads sponsored by the Indonesian army began slaughtering civilians in the island province of East Timor, the United Nations was willing to intervene, but only if asked to do so by the Indonesian government. An invitation would eliminate problems with national sovereignty.

The United States, the European Union, and the World Bank, among others, used economic pressure, such as threatening to withhold loans and foreign aid, to convince the Indonesian government to make that request. UN secretary-general Kofi Annan threatened Indonesian officials with prosecution for crimes against humanity if they did not permit a UN-sponsored force to enter East Timor. The Indonesians relented.

On June 11, 1999, the UN established the United Nations Mission in East Timor (UNAMET). Its job was to keep the peace and conduct free elections on East Timor's future. In August, the people voted to break their ties with Indonesia.

With the help of UNAMET and other agencies, the Timorese began working toward creating a new nation. The process was long and difficult. Finally, on March 22, 2002, eighty-eight Timorese leaders signed a new constitution that would establish a democratic government with strong human rights guarantees for all citizens. Formal and final independence from Indonesia occurred on May 20, 2002; the East Timorese people celebrated with fireworks and parades.

Controversy in Kosovo

In the Yugoslavian province of Kosovo, international intervention became more controversial than in East Timor. Kosovo had been almost entirely self-governing until Yugoslav president Slobodan Milosevic instituted martial law in 1989. This heightened ethnic tensions between Christian Serbs and Muslim ethnic Albanians in the province.

Ten years later, those tensions erupted into ethnic

warfare. When the killing started in 1998, the UN sent an unarmed group known as the Kosovo Verification Mission to calm the situation. For a time, it worked; the violence stopped.

Unfortunately, it began again in early 1999. UN-sponsored peace efforts failed. President Milosevic, himself a Serb, unleashed ethnic cleansing and mass murder against the ethnic Albanians of Kosovo. Many began to call for international military intervention in the situation.

This time, it was not the United Nations that responded, but NATO. Under the leadership of the United States, NATO launched a bombing campaign against Yugoslavia that lasted seventy-eight days.

At a refugee center in Macedonia in 1999, children receive their first hot meals after escaping from Kosovo. The British soldiers serving them are part of the multinational force sent by NATO.

The operation was highly controversial. The bombing lasted much longer than the operation in Bosnia, and there was a wider selection of targets. Many human rights activists worried about the risk to innocent civilians. Others questioned the wisdom of using violence in the name of peace. Human Rights Watch felt that NATO came dangerously close to violating "the principles of humanitarian action."[6]

Controversial though it was, the NATO bombardment produced results. On June 9, the Yugoslav government agreed to withdraw its troops from Kosovo and allow a United Nations peacekeeping force to enter.

Though NATO had accomplished its objectives in Kosovo, the controversy surrounding its methods continued. At the heart of that controversy lay the old issue of national sovereignty. Respect for each nation's right to conduct its own affairs within its own borders was the very foundation of international law. Changing that foundation, even in the name of human rights, will be a difficult task. It is likely to become a central issue of the twenty-first century.

International Justice

Another important task will be developing a system of international justice to deal with tyrants who commit crimes against humanity. Activists are working on two levels: confronting issues of jurisdiction, or legal authority, in matters of human rights and creating an international criminal court to deal with human rights violators anywhere in the world.

Jurisdiction is an important principle of law. The issues can become complex and confusing, but the basic idea is fairly simple: Legal systems can only prosecute crimes committed in their defined areas of authority. Some human rights activists contend that there should be an exception for crimes against humanity. For example, Human Rights Watch favors a limited principle of "universal jurisdiction," based on the idea that some crimes "so offend humankind . . . that courts anywhere have [lawful authority] to try them."[7]

Spain tested the limits of jurisdiction in October 1998, when it brought charges against Augusto Pinochet, former dictator of Chile. Spanish authorities based their claim to jurisdiction on the charge that Pinochet had killed and persecuted Spanish citizens living in Chile. By international standards, this was a weak argument for jurisdiction. Many human rights activists regarded the Pinochet matter as a test case for the principle of universal jurisdiction. Human Rights Watch called it "a wake-up call for tyrants around the world."[8]

Certainly, Pinochet's dictatorship in Chile had offended the conscience of millions around the world. During his seventeen years in power (1973–1990), Pinochet turned the small South American country into a brutal police state. Thousands were tortured or killed; thousands more lived in terror for their lives.

Pinochet never stood trial in Spain. After sixteen months in British custody, he was freed on the grounds of poor health and allowed to return to

Chile. The eighty-four-year-old former dictator was afflicted with high blood pressure, diabetes, and arthritis.

Chilean authorities brought their own charges against Pinochet. After a lengthy legal battle, the charges were suspended on the grounds that Pinochet was medically unfit to stand trial.

Despite this outcome, many human rights activists considered the fact that Pinochet was even charged with crimes to be a partial victory. During and after the Pinochet case, other tyrants suddenly found themselves facing charges. For example, the United Nations established the International Criminal Tribunal for Former Yugoslavia. Among many other actions, this tribunal indicted President Slobodan Milosevic for his actions in Kosovo. This gave Milosevic the dubious distinction of becoming the first sitting head of state to be charged with crimes against humanity.

A similar UN tribunal for Rwanda indicted a number of leaders for genocide and other crimes, primarily against the Tutsi minority. By the end of 1999, five had been convicted, including former prime minister Jean Kambanda.

Tribunals such as those for Rwanda and Yugoslavia are temporary organizations. When their work is done, they disband. In 1992, a Commission of the United Nations began creating a statute for a permanent International Criminal Court (ICC).

Unlike the existing World Court, which hears disputes between nations rather than criminal cases, the ICC would have international jurisdiction over individuals accused of such offenses as war crimes, crimes against humanity, and genocide. The ICC could bring criminal charges against these individuals, place them on trial, and set punishment for those found guilty.

On July 17, 1998, in Rome, Italy, 160 nations participated in a conference. They voted overwhelmingly in favor of what came to be known as the Rome Statute. This vote did not establish the ICC. It merely authorized a ratification, or confirmation, process. In order to create the court, sixty member nations had to ratify the Rome Statute.

Ratification is a complex and usually lengthy process. In most countries, it requires approval by the national legislature. On March 21, 2002, Panama became the fifty-sixth nation to ratify the Rome Statute. Many nations, including the United States, have refused to ratify the ICC in its present form, because of concern over national sovereignty issues.

Human Rights in the Twenty-first Century

The fate of the International Criminal Court and other efforts to establish a worldwide legal system will largely depend upon the willingness of governments to accept some limits to national sovereignty. Nations would have to agree that under certain conditions, international law would take precedence, or go before, the laws of any country. This would be a big step, even in cases where the basic issue is fairly clear.

For example, the international community has largely agreed that a nation's right to conduct its own affairs in its own way should not extend to the "right" to commit genocide. Unfortunately, this does not mean that the United Nations or some other international body could simply pass a law against genocide and be done with it.

The picture gets complicated when issues of enforcement come into play. Who decides what is and what is not genocide, and on what basis do they make that decision? What agency would have the right to take action against a genocidal government and what forms could that action take? How would the guilty be brought to justice? How could they be punished for their crimes, and who would have authority to impose that punishment? These are not easy questions to answer.

Derived Rights

Genocide is an obvious violation of the most basic human right of all: the right to life itself. The famous guarantee of "life, liberty and the pursuit of happiness" in the U.S. Constitution states rights that are considered to apply to all people at all times and in all places. The United Nations' Universal Declaration of Human Rights does the same, phrasing it as "the right to life, liberty, and security of person."

Derived rights are those which grow out of specifically stated rights. For example, a right to adequate food, shelter, and medical care can be derived from the right to life.

Few would disagree that in a just world, all people should be entitled to the means of life. However, there are those who question whether the obligation to provide them should be given the force of international law. Such a law would be difficult to enforce, and poorer nations might lack the resources to obey it.

Some activists have similar concerns about highly detailed legal codes in general. They believe that a law that is limited to broad issues in human rights would have a better chance of acceptance by the international community and be more enforceable once enacted. Others argue that human rights is a developing idea which must be allowed to grow. New laws should be added when the need for them becomes clear.

This debate is likely to be important for some time to come. The issues are significant, and there are sound arguments on both sides.

Other important issues at the beginning of the twenty-first century include children's rights, the death penalty, the right to privacy, and the need to balance the security concerns of nations with the rights of individuals. None of these issues are new. However, they have acquired new importance due to world events.

Children's Rights

Children's rights begin with the realization that children are human beings in their own right, and not the "property" of their parents. In 1989, the United

Nations set an international standard with the Convention on the Rights of the Child.

Many people think that the Convention applies only to children in poor countries—children who are starving, enslaved, homeless, or victims of war and civil strife. Actually, children everywhere need its protections. For example, child abuse is a major problem in the United States. So is violence in the schools. Authorities have to protect children from other children, and they have to do it without violating anyone's civil rights.

Until 1967, American children accused of crimes did not have the same rights as adults. The case of

This little girl was photographed in the North Carolina mill where she was working in 1912. Though child labor is forbidden by law in the United States, there are many countries where children still work in dangerous conditions for little pay.

fifteen-year-old Gerald Gault changed that. Gault was accused of making an obscene phone call to a neighbor. In a juvenile court hearing, the judge found the boy "delinquent" and sent him to a state institution until he turned twenty-one. An adult convicted of the same offense would have served two months in county jail or paid a fine of no more than $50.

The Gault case went all the way to the Supreme Court. By ruling in Gault's favor, the Court established the principle that a child accused of a crime was entitled to the same legal rights as an adult. These rights include trial by jury, representation by a lawyer, and protection against cruel or unusual punishment if convicted.

By the beginning of the twenty-first century, children's rights had become a high priority in nations all over the world. Many obstacles remained. Children in some parts of the world still lived in slavery. Many were starving or dying of epidemic disease. Many more were victims of war; some were even used as soldiers. Saving these victims and protecting all children will be a challenge for many years to come.

The Death Penalty

The death penalty is an example of an issue that has received fresh attention. It has long been both controversial and emotional. People care passionately on both sides.

Those who favor the death penalty argue that fear

of it helps to prevent the most serious crimes. Some also point out that it is the one way to be sure that the most vicious criminals will never harm anyone again.

Opponents argue that the death penalty is "cruel and unusual" punishment that violates the basic right to life. They dispute the argument that fear of the death penalty prevents crime.

In 1999, the UN Commission on Human Rights came down strongly on the side of death penalty opponents. It called upon all nations to restrict the number of crimes for which the death penalty may be imposed, with the aim of abolishing it totally. By January 2001, more than half the nations in the world had done away with the death penalty entirely or at least suspended all executions.

The Right to Privacy

Advances in computer and communications technology and especially the explosive growth of the Internet in the 1990s have raised concerns about personal privacy. Government and police agencies have access to surveillance equipment that can monitor a person's every move. Some of this equipment can literally see and hear through closed doors. Various official agencies as well as private companies and even individuals can build amazingly detailed profiles by tracking a person's activity on the Internet.

This information can be used in many ways, not all of them honest. Misuse of the Internet has helped to produce a new crime: identity theft. Unscrupulous persons amass enough information on a particular individual to pose as that person. They can apply for credit, charge purchases, even use the victim's education and employment history as their own.

Governments can do even worse. It is no accident that in the most brutal dictatorships, the right of privacy is one of the first to be endangered. Long before present surveillance equipment existed, police states used such things as informers, spies, and secret investigations to invade people's private lives. Modern technology gives this invasion of privacy an efficiency that is frightening to supporters of human rights.

Human Rights and the War on Terrorism

Privacy, along with many other rights, became a concern in the United States after the terrorist attacks of September 11, 2001. The United States, with support from many nations, launched a war on terrorism. On October 8, 2001, President George W. Bush established a new Office of Homeland Security to protect against future terrorist activity within the United States.

America began a struggle to balance the need for greater national security with the need to protect the rights of individuals. The issues are difficult. For example, the terrorists of September 11 were Arabs, members of a group headed by Muslim extremist Osama bin Laden. They turned commercial jetliners into weapons of destruction. Does that justify special questioning of airline passengers who appear to be Arabs or who have Arabic names?

On September 11, 2001, terrorists flew a plane into the World Trade Center in New York City, destroying the building and killing thousands of people. This attack, along with others at the same time in Washington, D.C., and Pennsylvania, raised questions about the balance between national security and individual rights.

From the standpoint of national security, the answer may well be yes, at least with careful regulation to avoid abuses. From the standpoint of individual rights, the answer is not quite so clear. By their very nature, such policies single out people because of their racial, ethnic, or religious identity. While this may be necessary, it is also risky. To prevent the war on terrorism from becoming a setback for human rights, authorities must work to balance the need to protect society as a whole with the need to safeguard individual rights.

Human Rights: Past, Present, and Future

Concepts of human rights and the legal codes supporting them have changed over time. By today's standards, the "eye for an eye" philosophy of the Code of Hammurabi sounds harsh. Its punishments appear excessive or even barbaric. On the other hand, the Universal Declaration of Human Rights would have sounded incredibly strange in Hammurabi's time.

Some of today's issues and answers may sound equally strange to people of the future. Some may be all too familiar. Human history is not a record of unbroken progress over time. For example, the Emancipation Proclamation of 1863 abolished slavery in the United States. Yet today, African Americans still face discrimination in many forms. Slavery still exists in Sudan and many other parts of the world.

Will slavery exist, perhaps in different forms and other places, 150 years from now? What issues will grow out of technological advances and social change? Of course, no one knows the answer to these questions.

New issues will arise and old ones will resurface, perhaps in forms that people today cannot even imagine. Underneath it all, at least one thing will remain the same: Preserving, protecting, and developing human rights will continue to require the efforts of people of good will everywhere in the world.

Chapter Notes

Chapter 1. Human Rights: What They Are and Why They Matter

1. "The Slave Experience," *iAbolish: The Anti-Slavery Portal*, 2001, <http://iabolish.com/today/experience/mental.htm> (March 11, 2002).

2. William Lloyd Garrison, "To the Public," *The Liberator*, January 1, 1831, <http://www.pbs.org/wgbh/aia/part4/4h2928t.html> (May 22, 2001).

3. Henry David Thoreau, "Civil Disobedience," in *Henry David Thoreau: Collected Essays and Poems* (New York: Library of America, 2001), p. 213.

Chapter 2. The Foundations of Human Rights

1. "The Code of Hammurabi," L.W. King, translator (Las Vegas: World Library, 1996), #196, Screen 37.

2. Ibid.

3. Nathan Ausubel, *The Book of Jewish Knowledge* (New York: Crown Publishers, 1964), p. 193.

4. J.F. Watts, *Seven Cultural Traditions* (New York: Simon and Schuster, 1994), pp. 405–409, <http://www.ccny.cuny.edu/humanities/history/reader/romanlaw.htm> (February 18, 2002).

5. "Roman Law," *The Catholic Encyclopedia*, n.d., <http://www.newadvent.org./cathen/09079a.htm> (March 12, 2002).

6. Michael Palumbo, *Human Rights: Meaning and History* (Malabar, Fla.: Robert E. Krieger Publishing Company, 1982), p. 22.

Chapter 3. Rights and Revolutions

1. George Hewes, "Boston Tea Party," *The History Place*, n.d., <http://ahp.gatech.edu/tea_party_account_1773.html> (March 12, 2002).

2. Eric Foner, *The Story of American Freedom* (New York: W.W. Norton & Co., 1998), p. 16.

3. Michael Palumbo, *Human Rights: Meaning and History* (Malabar, Fla.: Robert E. Krieger Publishing Company, 1982), p. 120.

Chapter 4. The Struggle Against Slavery

1. Hugh Thomas, *The Slave Trade* (New York: Simon & Schuster, 1997), p. 21.

2. "Opening Statement to the House Judiciary Committee on Impeachment of Richard Nixon," *A Tribute to Barbara Jordan (1936–1996)*, n.d., <http://www.elf.net/bjordan/judiciary.html> (May 15, 2001).

3. Thomas, p. 490.

4. Eric Foner, *The Story of American Freedom* (New York: W.W. Norton & Co., 1998), p. 95.

5. Leon F. Litwack, *Trouble in Mind: Black Southerners in the Age of Jim Crow* (New York: Alfred A. Knopf, 1998), p. xiii.

Chapter 5. In Time of War

1. Dennis Niemiec and Shawn Windsor, "Arab Americans expect scrutiny, feel sting of bias," *Detroit Free Press*, October 1, 2001, <http://www.freep.com/news/nw/terror2001/poll1_20011001.htm> (March 15, 2002).

2. "Frequently Asked Questions about the Armenian Genocide," *Armenian National Institute Page*, 1998–2001, <http://www.armenian-genocide.org/genocidefaq.htm> (March 15, 2002).

3. Donald E. Miller and Lorna Touryan Miller, *Survivors: An Oral History of the Armenian Genocide* (Berkeley, Calif.: University of California Press, 1993), p. 41.

4. James Mace, "The Man-Made Famine of 1932–1933: What Happened and Why," *The Great*

Famine in Ukraine: The Unknown Holocaust (Jersey City, N.J.: Ukranian National Association, 1988), p. 29.

5. Ibid., p. 84.

6. Michael Burleigh, *The Third Reich: A New History* (New York: Hill and Wang, 2000), p. 152.

7. General Assembly of the United Nations. "Universal Declaration of Human Rights," December 10, 1948, <http://www.un.org/Overview/rights.html> (June 15, 2001).

8. Ibid.

Chapter 6. Human Rights and Civil Disobedience

1. Henry David Thoreau, "Civil Disobedience," in *Henry David Thoreau: Collected Essays and Poems* (New York: Library of America, 2001), p. 204.

2. Louis Fischer, *Gandhi: His Life and Message for the World* (New York: New American Library, 1954), p. 38.

3. Mohandas K. Gandhi, *Gandhi: An Autobiography* (Boston: Beacon Press, 1957), p. 318.

4. Fischer, p. 109.

5. Martin Luther King, Jr., *Stride Toward Freedom: The Montgomery Story* (New York: Harper and Brothers, 1986), p. 91.

6. Ibid., p. 96.

7. Ibid., p. 91.

8. Ibid., p. 97.

9. Ibid., p. 102.

Chapter 7. The Activist Sixties

1. Todd Gitlin, *The Sixties: Years of Hope, Days of Rage* (New York: Bantam Books, revised 1993), p. 145.

2. Ibid., p. 146.

3. Eric Foner, *The Story of American Freedom* (New York: W.W. Norton & Co., 1998), p. 290.

4. Edward Lazarus, *Black Hills, White Justice: The Sioux Nation Versus the United States 1775 to the Present* (New York: HarperCollins Publishers, 1991), p. 291.

5. Ibid., p. 290.

6. Lyndon B. Johnson, "Proposal for a Nationwide War on the Sources of Poverty," Message to Congress, March 16, 1964, *Internet Modern History Sourcebook*, <http://www.fordham.edu/halsall/mod/1964johnson-warpoverty.html> (June 25, 2001).

7. Ibid.

8. Lyndon Baines Johnson, "The Great Society," Speech delivered May 22, 1964, *The Program in Presidential Rhetoric*, <http://www.tamu.edu/scom/pres/speeches/lbjgreat.html> (May 25, 2001).

9. Matthew Frost, "Czech Republic: A Chronology of Events Leading to the 1968 Invasion," *Radio Free Europe/Radio Liberty*, 1998, <http://www.rferl.org/nca/features/1998/08/F.RU.980820113706.html> (March 20, 2002).

10. "Czechoslovakia in 1968: An Invasion Remembered," *Radio Free Europe/Radio Liberty*, 1995–1998, <http://www.rferl.org/nca/special/invasion1968> (March 20, 2002).

11. "Andrei Dmitrievich Sakharov: biography," *Andrei Sakharov Foundation Page*, n.d., <http://www.wdn.com/asf/adsbio.html> (March 21, 2002).

Chapter 8. The New Internationalism

1. "Foreign Aid and Human Rights (1976)," *Basic Readings in U.S. Democracy*, n.d., <http://usinfo.state.gov/usa/infousa/facts/democrac/54.htm> (July 2, 2001).

2. *Model Curriculum for Human Rights and Genocide* (Sacramento, Calif.: California State Department of Education, 1988), p. 59.

3. Ibid., p. 61.

4. Ibid., pp. 56–57.

5. Anthony Sampson, *Mandela: The Authorized Biography* (New York: Alfred A. Knopf, 1999), p. 187.

6. "The History of Apartheid in South Africa: The Ethical Questions Posed for the International Community," *Stanford University Computer Science Department Page*, n.d., <http://www-cs-students.stanford.edu/~cale/cs201/apartheid.ethics.html> (July 2, 2001).

7. "Video Almanac 1989: Chinese government thwarts democracy movement," *CNN Interactive*, June 3, 1989, <http://207.25.71.25/resources/video.almanac/1989/index2.html#tiananmen> (May 17, 2002).

8. Zhang Liang, compiler, Andrew J. Nathan and Perry Link, eds., *The Tiananmen Papers* (New York: Public Affairs, 2001), p. 436.

9. Ibid., p. 381.

10. Ibid., p. 455.

Chapter 9. Unfinished Business

1. Zlata Filipović, *Zlata's Diary: A Child's Life in Sarajevo* (New York: Viking Books, 1994), pp. 102–103.

2. Maud S. Beelman, *Internal Displacement, Crimes of War Project: The Book*, n.d., <http://www.crimesofwar.org/thebook/internal-displacement.html> (March 23, 2002).

3. Joint Evaluation of Emergency Assistance to Rwanda, "The International Response to Conflict and Genocide: Lessons from the Rwandan Experience," *Journal of Humanitarian Assistance*, April 14, 1996, <http://www.jha.ac/> (May 16, 2002)

4. Ibid.

5. Human Rights Watch, *World Report 2000,* December 1999, <http://www.hrw.org/wr2k/Front.htm> (July 7, 2001).

6. Ibid.

7. Ibid.

8. Ibid.

Glossary

autonomous—Independent, self-governing.

code—A systematized body of law or principles.

communism—A form of government in which all property is owned by the people in common.

compensate—To make amends; to pay or reimburse (as for damages).

concentration camp—A prison camp for political prisoners and other noncriminals.

death march—A forced migration, or movement, in which abuse and bad conditions will cause many deaths.

decree—A formal order or decision.

dictator—A person with absolute powers of government, especially an oppressor.

divine right (of kings)—The belief that monarchs rule by the will of God.

ethnic cleansing—The elimination of an unwanted group from a society, as by forced migration or mass killing.

expulsion—To be driven out by force.

extradition—The surrender of an accused person or fugitive by one nation or jurisdiction to another.

forced migration—Compelling large numbers of people to leave their homes and go to a new location.

genocide—The deliberate and systematic destruction of a racial, political, or cultural group.

inalienable—That which cannot rightfully be taken away.

internal displacement—To be forced out of home, yet remain in the same country.

jurisdiction—Lawful right to exercise authority, as in a given area.

martial law—Rule by military forces when civil authority has broken down.

motive—A need or drive that causes a person to engage in some action or behavior.

natural rights—Those rights that belong to all persons from birth.

nongovernmental organizations (NGOs)—Privately funded groups that owe allegiance to no particular nation.

North Atlantic Treaty Organization (NATO)—An alliance of Western democracies, formed for mutual support and military defense.

poll tax—A tax paid at the voting place in order to qualify to vote.

prosecute—To carry out a legal proceeding; for example, a criminal trial.

province—A country or territory incorporated into and governed by a larger nation or empire.

refugee—One who flees to another country to escape danger or persecution.

secede—To withdraw formally from an association, particularly a political or religious organization.

sovereignty—The state of being self-governing and independent of outside interference.

surveillance—The act of keeping close watch over someone or something.

totalitarian—Rule by one party or faction by repression.

treaty—A formal agreement between two or more states.

Warsaw Pact—An alliance involving the former Soviet Union and several Eastern European states, formed for mutual support and military defense.

Further Reading

Books

Archer, Jules. *They Had a Dream: The Civil Rights Struggle From Frederick Douglass to Marcus Garvey to Martin Luther King and Malcolm X*. New York: Puffin, 1996.

Denenberg, Barry. *Nelson Mandela: No Easy Walk to Freedom*. New York: Scholastic Trade, 1991.

Hitt, Laura, ed. *Human Rights (Great Speeches in History)*. San Diego, Calif.: Greenhaven Press, 2001.

Kuklin, Susan. *Irrepressible Spirit: Conversations With Human Rights Activists*. New York: Philomel Books, 1996.

Severance, John B. *Gandhi Great Soul*. Boston, Mass.: Houghton Mifflin Co., 1957.

Springer, Jane. *Listen to Us: The World's Working Children*. Toronto, Canada: Groundwood Books, 1998.

Internet Addresses

Human Rights Watch
<http://www.hrw.org/>

United Nations Human Rights
<http://www.un.org/rights/>

World Policy Institute: Americas Project
<http://www.worldpolicy.org/americas/
usaindex.html>

Index

A

abolitionists, 39–42
abortion, 82–83
African Americans, 38–39,
    42–46, 72, 73
Alcatraz Island, 76, 77
American Indian
    Movement (AIM), 76
American Indians, 25, 75,
    76
American Revolution, 27,
    28
Amnesty International, 86
Annan, Kofi, 104
apartheid, 72, 92–93, 95
Arab Americans, 48
Argentina, 87, 91–92
Armenian Genocide,
    49–51

B

Baker, Ella, 72
Bastille, storming of, 32
Berkeley free speech move-
    ment, 74
Bill of Rights, American,
    30, 31–32
bin Laden, Osama, 115
Bok, Francis, 7–8
Bolsheviks, 52
Bonaparte, Napoleon, 33,
    34
Bosnia-Herzegovina,
    100–102
Boston Tea Party, 26–27
Buddha, 24

Bush, George W., 115

C

Cambodia, 87, 90–91
Carter, Jimmy, 89–90
caste system, 64–66
Chavez, Cesar, 75–76
children's rights, 111–113
Chile, 107–108
Christianity, 20–21
civil rights movement,
    66–68, 70, 72, 73
Civil War, American,
    42–43
Collingswood, Captain
    Luke, 40
Communism, 47, 51–54
Confucius, 24
counterculture, 74–75

D

death penalty, 9, 113–114
Declaration of
    Independence, 29–30
Declaration of the Rights
    of Man and of the
    Citizen, 32–33
democracy, 17, 28, 30
derived rights, 110–111
divine right of kings,
    27–28

E

East Timor, 103–104
English Bill of Rights,
    27–28
ethnic cleansing, 9, 101

F
feudalism, 21, 35
Filipovic, Zlata, 101
Foreign Assistance Act of
    1961, 88
French Revolution, 32–34

G
Gandhi, Mohandas K., 9,
    60, 61, 62–66, 75
Garrison, William Lloyd, 8,
    41–42
Gault, Gerald, 113
genocide, 49–50, 57, 110
Gitlin, Todd, 73
Glorious Revolution,
    27–28
Gorbachev, Mikhail, 84
Great Society, 77, 78
Greece, 17

H
Hammurabi, 13–15
Helsinki Accords, 87–88
Hitler, Adolf, 9, 54–56
Holocaust, 57
Human Rights Watch,
    86–87, 103, 106
Humphrey, Hubert H., 81
Hutu, 102

I
identity theft, 114–115
Indian independence,
    62–64, 66
Indonesia, 103–104
International Criminal
    Court (ICC), 108–109
Islam, 24–25

J
James II of England,
    27–28
Japanese Americans, 48
Jefferson, Thomas, 28

Jesus, 20
Jewish law, 15–16
Jim Crow (racial segrega-
    tion laws), 45–46
Johnson, Lyndon B., 77,
    78, 81
Jordan, Barbara, 39
jurisdiction (in law), 107
jus gentium, 19–20

K
Khmer Rouge, 90–91
King, Martin Luther, Jr., 9,
    60, 61, 66–68, 70,
    73, 75
Kosovo, 104–106

L
law
    Code of Hammurabi,
        13–15, 117
    Greek, 17
    Jewish, 15–16
    Napoleonic Code,
        33–35
    Roman, 19–20
lex talionis, 14, 16
Lincoln, Abraham, 42
Locke, John, 28
Louis XVI of France, 33

M
Madison, James, 31
Magna Carta, 22, 24
Mandela, Nelson, 92–93,
    95
McCarthy, Eugene, 81
McGovern, George, 81
medieval Europe, 21–22,
    24
Mexican Americans, 75–76
Montgomery bus boycott,
    67–68
Muhammad, 24

N

Nazi Party, 54–57
Ninth Amendment, 31–32
Nixon, Richard, 81
nongovernmental organizations (NGOs), 86–87
North Atlantic Treaty Organization (NATO), 87–88, 105–106
Nuremberg Trials, 57

P

Parks, Rosa, 67
People's Republic of China, 96–98
Pinochet, Augusto, 107–108
Prague Spring, 72, 83
privacy, right to, 9, 11, 114–115

R

racism, 38–39, 45–46
Roe v. *Wade*, 82
Roman Catholic Church, 21, 22
Roman Empire, 19–20, 21
Rwanda, 102–103

S

Sakharov, Andrei, 72, 84
slavery, 7–8, 9, 30, 31, 36–44, 61, 117
South Africa, 87, 92–93, 95
Soviet Union, 51–54
Stalin, Joseph, 9, 53, 54
Student Nonviolent Coordinating Committee (SNCC), 72
Students for a Democratic Society (SDS), 73

T

Tenth Amendment, 31–32
terrorism, 11, 115–116
Thoreau, Henry David, 8, 60, 61–62, 63, 67
Tiananmen Square, 96–98
Timerman, Jacobo, 91
Truth and Reconciliation Commission, 95
Tutsi, 102

U

Ukrainian famine, 53–54
United Nations, 8, 51, 58, 72, 87, 93, 95, 100, 103, 104, 105, 108, 110, 111–112
Universal Declaration of Human Rights, 58–59, 117
Untouchables, 64–66

V

Vietnam, 79
Vietnam War, 79–81
Volunteers In Service To America (VISTA), 78

W

War on Poverty, 77–79
war on terrorism, 115–116
Warsaw Pact, 87
women's movement, 81–83
World Court, 108

Y

Yugoslavia, 100–102, 104–106

Z

Zong, 40–41